A PRACTICAL GUIDE TO ACCOUNTING BY CHARITIES

New Accounting Regulations and the revised SORP

by Kate Sayer

A Directory of Social Change Publication

A PRACTICAL GUIDE TO ACCOUNTING BY CHARITIES

New Accounting Regulations
and the revised SORP

by Kate Sayer

Copyright 1996 © The Directory of Social Change.
First published 1996. Reprinted 1997.

Form on pages 68–73 © Crown copyright 1996.
Reproduced by permission of Her Majesty's
Stationery Office.

Published by the Directory of Social Change
24 Stephenson Way
London NW1 2DP
Tel: 0171 209 5151, fax: 0171 209 5049
e-mail:info@d-s-c.demom.co.uk
from whom further copes and a full publications list are
available.

Directory of Social Change is a registered charity no.
800517.

Typeset by Diarmuid Burke
Printed and bound by Page Bros., Norwich

British Library Cataloguing in Publication Data
A catalogue record for this book is available from the
British Library

ISBN 1-873860-95-1

Other Directory of Social Change departments:
Courses and Conferences tel: 0171 209 4949
Charityfair tel: 0171 209 1015
Charity Centre tel: 0171 209 0902
Research tel: 0171 209 4422

Directory of Social Change Northern Office:
Federation House, Hope Street, Liverpool L1 9BW
Courses and Conferences tel: 0151 708 0117
Research tel: 0151 708 0136

Information About the Author

Kate Sayer is a partner in Sayer Vincent, a firm of chartered accountants and registered auditors that works only in the voluntary sector. Kate has been working with charities and not-for-profit organisations since 1984. Most of her time is spent working with charity clients on their audit, accounts and advising them on the many legal and financial issues which confront charities on a daily basis.

She has developed training and materials specially designed for those working in the charity sector, in particular non-accountants needing to understand and control the financial elements of management.

Kate is the author of two other highly-praised books in this series:

A Practical Guide to PAYE for Charities (1995)
"Clear and concise... an excellent guide." (Company Accountant)

A Practical Guide to VAT for Charities (1992)
"This book should be mandatory reading for finance staff." (Third Sector)

Both books are published by and available from the Directory of Social Change.

Acknowledgements

I am extemely grateful to many people who helped with the preparation of this book. Firstly, I would thank John Bonds, Charity Commissioner, for his support, encouragement and for his Foreword. A number of the accountants at the Charity Commission helped me with their comments and suggestions on the text. Greyham Dawes gave me detailed comments on the text and his time, for which I am very grateful. Ken Ashford and Ray Jones also gave me valuable assistance.

Graeme Thom of Scott-Moncrieff Chartered Accountants, Edinburgh gave me a great of information on the regulations applicable to Scottish Charities. Andrew Dobson also read and commented on the text for the chapter on Scottish charities. I am grateful to them both, especially for their tolerance in dealing with an ignorant southerner!

I have also received welcome support from Age Concern England, with encouragement from Keith Mastin and comments from Roger Paschley.

Sheila MacAlpine of the Auditing Practices Board was extremeful helpful at a time when I thought I might give up the attempt to reconcile the different demands of company law, charity law and Financial Reporting Standards!

The Council of Barnardo's kindly gave their permission for the reproduction of the charity's annual report for the year ended 31 March 1995.

I always receive lots of support and encouragement from my colleagues at Sayer Vincent. My thanks to Nicola Anderson, Pam Craig and Andy Gillies for reading and commenting on the draft. Many thanks to Michele for typing the example accounts and patiently coping with repeated amendments to them!

Contents

Foreword by John Bonds, Charity Commissioner 7

Introduction 9

Glossary 11

CHAPTER 1: The Legal Framework 15
- ◆ Charities Act 1993 – accounting and audit requirements
- ◆ The accounting regulations – when they apply and to whom
- ◆ Charitable companies

CHAPTER 2: The Annual Report 23
- ◆ Minimum requirements under the accounting regulations
- ◆ Detailed recommendations of the SORP
- ◆ Examples from charity annual reports.

CHAPTER 3: Overview of Best Practice 39
- ◆ Statement of Financial Activities
- ◆ Fund accounting
- ◆ Key terms in SORP
- ◆ Overview of main points

CHAPTER 4: Receipts and Payments Basis 57
- ◆ Example accounts for a small charity choosing to prepare a
  receipts and payments account and summary of assets and liabilities

CHAPTER 5: Small Charity Accounts – Accruals Basis 74
- ◆ Example accounts and explanatory notes for a charity with less
  than £100,000 gross income preparing accounts under the SORP

CHAPTER 6: Medium Sized Charity 86
- ◆ Example accounts and explanatory notes for a charity with
  approximately £270,000 gross income

CHAPTER 7: Larger Charity 108
- ◆ Example accounts for a charity with £1.3m gross income and
  a trading subsidiary preparing group accounts

CHAPTER 8: Audit 138
- ◆ Scope of audit and how affected by SORP
- ◆ Duties of auditors, special audit matters arising from SORP
- ◆ Example audit reports
- ◆ Whistleblowing
- ◆ Report on summarised accounts

CHAPTER 9: Independent Examinations 157
- ◆ Who may be an independent examiner
- ◆ What the independent examination involves
- ◆ What the report should say
- ◆ Guidance to charity trustees on choosing an independent examiner
- ◆ Examiner's work programme

CHAPTER 10: Scotland and Northern Ireland 171
- ◆ Auditing and accounting requirements in Scotland
- ◆ Example formats for accounts
- ◆ Example audit reports
- ◆ Draft legislation for Northern Ireland

Appendix 184
- ◆ Checklist for the notes to the accounts

Reference Materials 190

Index 191

FOREWORD

by John Bonds, Charity Commissioner

The Accounting Regulations have been signed; the Charities SORP has been published. So it is all go now with the regulations coming into effect with accounting periods starting on or after 1 March 1996. There is therefore plenty of time for charities to prepare themselves for producing accounts in the required manner and I am glad to say that many are already doing so and are seeing the benefits to be obtained. I therefore welcome this book produced by the Directory of Social Change in order to help charities with the new requirements. It is particularly refreshing to see how many people are tackling them with such enthusiasm and determination and this book should contribute to that process.

There has been some criticism about how long everything has taken, but it should be remembered that part of the delay resulted from the deregulation initiative and we should all be thankful for the much more reasonable thresholds which resulted from that (i.e. the thresholds for the levels at which accrual accounts are prepared and audit is required). On top of that, as a result of last year's consultation exercise and representations made, it was decided to extend the implementation date from 1 December 1995 to 1 March 1996 mainly in order to give time to those charities with branches to adapt themselves to the new requirements.

Following comments received during the consultation exercise, certain steps were taken by the Home Office and the Charity Commission to modify some of the draft proposals and make things easier for smaller charities (with income up to £100,000 per year). These charities will not be required to give a functional analysis of their expenditure (direct charitable expenditure/ fundraising and publicity/managing and administering the charity) but can analyse their expenditure as they consider appropriate. They will also not have to report departures from accounting standards and they will be able to produce a briefer annual report than that required from larger charities. Kate Sayer, author of this book, was one of those who contributed to the changes made and I am most grateful to her for her help.

The consultation exercise also revealed a lack of clarity on the expenditure headings and the opportunity was taken to reduce them from five to three and define them more clearly.

One of the questions regularly asked is the status of the SORP. It is sometimes misleadingly stated that the SORP is purely a set of recommendations which charities are free to adopt or reject as they feel like it.

The following, however, should be remembered:

1. The SORP is the basis for the Accounting Regulations (Part VI of the 1993 Charities Act) and does not simply consist of recommendations. If a charity follows the SORP, it will also be following the regulations.

2. The SORP is essential in interpreting the regulations not only because of the cross-references but also because it provides definitions which

are not given in the regulations, e.g. on expenditure headings, different fund classifications, recognition of liabilities, etc.

3. Where accounts are prepared on the accruals basis, charities (both incorporated and unincorporated) will have to follow the SORP in order to present a "true and fair view" of their state of affairs.

4. At the front of the SORP it is stated that the Charity Commissioners expect the accounts of charities and their accounting practices to comply fully with the SORP.

I hope these points will be remembered and charities will concentrate on the SORP rather than work from the regulations.

The SORP is admittedly complex at first sight. For that reason dispensations have been made for small charities as mentioned above and the Charity Commission is issuing two guides for those charities:

(i) A guide on the preparation of receipts and payments accounts.

(ii) A guide for charities with income of less than £100,000 who decide, or who are required by their funders, to prepare accounts on the accruals basis. This is called the Mini-SORP; it is not an alternative to the SORP but is simply a condensed version cutting out some of the SORP's more complicated features.

The Charity Commission will also do what it can to assist charities in interpreting the new requirements and for this purpose an accounts helpline has been established at our Liverpool office. We are also dependent on others in helping us to explain things and take the mystery out of the SORP. Most charities are only affected by parts of the SORP and not the whole of it. When this is realised, it becomes much less daunting.

This book should be of considerable help in making things clearer and getting people to understand what is required. It is therefore an important part of the process of improving standards in both the accounting and accountability of charities.

John Bonds
Commissioner

INTRODUCTION

This book is designed for all those involved with charity accounting who will need to apply the concepts and recommendations of the Statement of Recommended Practice: Accounting by Charities (SORP) and the accounting regulations for charities introduced by the Charities Act 1993.

It will not necessarily be an "easy read" for non-accountants trying to get to grips with foreign concepts and a different language. However, I would hope that the practical examples will demonstrate what is meant and what is required without too much reading of the theory.

This is also written for accountants, including auditors of charities and prospective independent examiners. It is not a substitute for reading the SORP itself or the valuable guides published by the Charity Commission. It is hoped rather that this book will throw some extra light on matters. If, at any point, there is an apparent contradiction, then please follow the SORP or the guides themselves.

The main focus of this book and the example accounts is the smaller charities. It does not cover the complex operations of very large charities. This is deliberate, as I am aware that the very large charities employ highly skilled accountants who will be able to produce excellent accounts without guidance from me. The largest example charity in this book is the one in Chapter 7, which has gross income of just over £1 million. Its operations are relatively complex, so this will be sufficient guidance for the majority of charities.

Because some of the matters covered in the SORP are new, we are bound to learn from experience. The example accounts represent "best practice" as we currently understand it and from my experience of preparing and auditing charity accounts for the last twelve years. This will no doubt change over the next few years as we need to respond to new forms of fundraising and charitable activity. The information presented here is current law and practice at March 1996.

Kate Sayer
March 1996

GLOSSARY

Accountant's Report
A report by a qualified accountant confirming that the accounts have been properly prepared. Also known as a compilation report – see Chapter 1 on companies.

Accounting Regulations
The regulations made under the Charities Act 1993. Full title: The Charities (Accounts and Reports) Regulations 1995. Sets out the statutory requirements for the form and content of charity accounts.

Accruals basis
This is a method of accounting which adjusts the receipts and payments for amounts which should have been collected or paid before the end of the accounting period to arrive at the income and expenditure account.

Assets
These are the money, goods and property which an organisation possesses, including any legal rights it may have to receive money, goods, services and property from others.

Balance Sheet
A summary of the assets and liabilities of an organisation at a particular date. Sometimes described as a "snapshot" of an organisation. It also describes the funds which are represented by the net assets.

Capital
The capital of a charity is a restricted fund (or funds) which the trustees must retain for the benefit of the charity and not spend.

Compilation report
A report by a qualified accountant on the accounts of a company to confirm that they have been properly prepared. An external review that is less than an audit and allowed under the audit exemption rules available to companies.

Designated funds
These are unrestricted funds which have been earmarked for a particular purpose by the trustees.

Direct charitable expenditure
This comprises all expenditure directly relating to the objects of the charity. It includes grants payable and the direct cost of supporting charitable activities and projects.

Endowment
An endowment is a special type of restricted fund which must be retained intact and not spent.

Expendable endowment
This is a type of endowment fund where trustees have the discretion to eventually convert the fund into spendable income.

Explanatory document
See "governing document" – term sometimes used by Scottish charities.

Financial Reporting Standard (FRS)	This is a statement issued by the Accounting Standards Board (ASB) to be followed in the preparation of all accounts. Whilst they do not have statutory force in themselves, they are referred to in company legislation and it is expected that all accounts will follow them if they are to show a true and fair view.
Financial statements	The accounts of an organisation including the notes to the accounts and any other statements which are required to be included.
Fixed assets	These are assets which continue to be of value to the organisation year after year and which the trustees hold on a long-term basis and therefore do not intend to dispose of in the short term.
Founding deed	See "governing document" – term sometimes used by Scottish charities.
Fundraising and publicity costs	These are the costs of obtaining funds for the charity's work, such as advertising, direct mail, staff time, agent's fees.
General funds	These are unrestricted funds which have not been earmarked and may be used generally to further the charity's stated objects.
Governing document	This is the document which establishes the charity and has to be passed by the Charity Commission prior to registration of the charity. It sets out the charity's objects and the rules of the organisation. It may be known by several different names: governing instrument; constitution; trust deed; Memorandum and Articles of Association (for a charitable company); Rules (for an Industrial and Provident Society); explanatory document (in Scotland); founding deed (in Scotland);
Gross income	Generally means all the income of an organisation for the financial year before deductions of any expenses. Specifically defined for the purposes of thresholds under the Charities Act to exclude all capital (endowment) incoming resources, sale of fixed assets, sale of investments.
Income and Expenditure Account	A summary of the income due and expenditure incurred for a financial year, showing the revenue transactions only.
Incoming resources	All resources available to a charity, including incoming capital (endowment), restricted income, gifts in kind and intangible income.

Independent examiner	An accountant or other competent person who is experienced in accounts who examines the accounts of a charity without performing an audit. A new provision under the Charities Act 1993 allows for charities below the £250,000 threshold to have an independent examination instead of an audit.
Liabilities	These are the amounts owed by an organisation at the balance sheet date. The cost will have already have been incurred, but the bill not paid.
Management and administration	These are the costs incurred in the management of the charity's assets, organisational administration and compliance with statutory requirements.
Permanent endowment	This is a type of endowment fund where the trustees must retain the fund intact as capital and use the funds to generate income or hold the assets (depending on the terms of the trust). The trustees have no discretion to convert the endowment into spendable income.
Receipts and Payments Account	A simple form of accounts which summarises the cash transactions of a charity. An option available to smaller charities.
Registered auditor	An accountant or firm of accountants who are registered to undertake company audits and are regulated in their work by one of the accountancy bodies.
Restricted fund	This is a fund subject to specific trusts within the objects of the charity (e.g. by a letter from the donor at the time of the gift, or by the terms of a public appeal). It may be a capital fund, which cannot be spent but must be retained for the benefit of the charity, or it may be an income fund, which must be spent on the specified purpose within a reasonable time.
Scottish charity	A body established in Scotland and recognised as charitable by the Inland Revenue.
SORP	see Statement of Recommended Practice
Statement of Assets and Liabilities	A summary required for charities preparing accounts under the receipts and payments basis. Not the same as a balance sheet; non-monetary assets do not have to be valued.
Statement of Financial Activities (SOFA)	New financial statement introduced especially for charities in the SORP. Summarises all incoming resources and application of resources. Replacing the income and expenditure account as a primary financial statement, it goes further by bringing together all the transactions of a charity. Described in full in Chapter 3.

Statement of Recommended Practice (SORP)	Guidance on the appropriate treatment of items in the accounts of specialised bodies.
Statement of Standard Accounting Practice (SSAP)	This is a statement issued by the Accounting Standards Board (ASB) to be followed in the preparation of all accounts. Whilst they do not have statutory force in themselves, they are referred to in company legislation and it is expected that all accounts will follow them if they are to show a true and fair view.
Support costs	These are part of the direct charitable expenditure and may be the management of projects from a central office. They may include a fair proportion of central office running costs.
Total expenditure	All the outgoings of an organisation for a financial year, excluding purchases of fixed assets and investments.
Unrestricted funds	These are funds held for the general purposes of the charity, to be spent within the stated objects.

Chapter 1

THE LEGAL BACKGROUND

Up until now, there has been no statutory requirement for charities to have an audit and only certain charities had to file annual accounts with the Charity Commission. Part VI of the Charities Act 1993 ("the Act") has introduced a number of changes affecting the audit and accounts of charities. In addition to that part of the Act, The Charities (Accounts and Reports) Regulations 1995 ("the accounting regulations") have been introduced which supplement the Act itself, and have statutory force. Part VI and the accounting regulations are effective for financial years commencing after 1 March 1996 and apply to charities in England and Wales only. Most of the provisions only apply to unincorporated charities, as charitable companies have to comply with the Companies Acts.

The 1993 Act strengthens the powers of the Charity Commission in relation to enforcement of accounting and audit requirements. The accounting regulations set out the form and content of accounts and the annual report; they also set out the duties of auditors and independent examiners.

The Statement of Recommended Practice (SORP) is not a statutory document, but accounts which should show a true and fair view will need to follow its recommendations. It represents current best practice and should be followed immediately by all charitable entities unless a more specialised SORP applies. The accounting regulations do invoke the SORP on some matters and the SORP provides some definitions which assist in the interpretation of the accounting regulations. The Charity Commissioners' introduction to the SORP makes it clear that they do expect all charities to follow the SORP. Auditors will also expect charities to follow the SORP and will refer to any departures from the SORP in their audit report, unless they think that the departures are required in order for the accounts to show a true and fair view. So whilst the SORP is not mandatory, charities will be expected to follow it.

The SORP and the accounting regulations have been developed in parallel. The accounting regulations are the skeleton whilst the SORP puts meat on the skeleton. If charities follow the SORP, then they will also comply with the accounting regulations.

Accounting Records

The Charities Act 1993 extends the provisions set out in the 1960 Charities Act in relation to the maintenance of accounting records and brings unincorporated charities broadly into line with company legislation. Section 41 does not apply to companies, but similar provisions are contained in the Companies Acts. Section 41 of the 1993 Act sets out:

- ◆ charities must keep accounting records to show and explain the charity's transactions
- ◆ the accounting records should contain day to day entries for all sums of money received or spent, showing the source or destination of funds
- ◆ charities must keep records of assets and liabilities
- ◆ you should be able to show with reasonable accuracy the charity's financial position on any particular date in the past
- ◆ accounting records must be kept for at least six years after the end of the financial year to which they relate

Section 41 applies to excepted charities, as well as charities below the £10,000 threshold. Exempt charities have to comply with sections 46(1) and 46(2), which requires that proper accounting records are kept. Thus, all charitable bodies must keep proper accounting records.

Annual Accounts

Prior to the 1993 Act, charities were obliged by law to prepare accounts, but only to submit these to the Charity Commission annually upon request or if the charity had permanent endowment. In addition, the form and content of the accounts of unincorporated charities was not prescribed in detail. After 1 March 1996 their accounts must be prepared in the prescribed form for each financial year. The prescribed form depends on the size of the charity and details of the form and content are set out in the accounting regulations.

The basic requirements are that charities must prepare a Statement of Financial Activities (SOFA), which replaces the income and expenditure account, and a Balance Sheet. The accounting regulations also specify explanatory notes which must accompany accounts and the categories in which items should be shown in the main statements. Small unincorporated charities may choose to prepare a receipts and payments account and a statement of assets and liabilities instead of full accruals accounts.

Annual Accounts – Summary of Requirements

All charities have to prepare a set of accounts each year.

"Light touch" regime for unincorporated charities with neither gross income nor total expenditure above £10,000 – accounts must be prepared but do not have to be submitted to the Charity Commission, unless requested.

Unincorporated charities with gross income up to £100,000 may choose to prepare accounts on the receipts and payments basis.

Charities with gross income above £100,000 must prepare accounts on the "accruals" basis. Exempt charities do not have to submit accounts to the Charity Commission at all.

Excepted charities only have to submit accounts to the Charity Commission if registered or if requested to do so.

Charitable companies are not affected by these provisions and have to follow the Companies Acts, but they do have to submit report and accounts to the Charity Commission.

Charities Not Exceeding the £100,000 Threshold

There are reliefs for smaller charities; unincorporated charities with gross income of not more than £100,000 may choose to prepare a simpler form of accounts comprising a receipts and payments account accompanied by a statement of assets and liabilities. This will be instead of the SOFA and Balance Sheet. The Charity Commission will accept the completion of their standard form (Form ACC-1371) instead of a separate set of accounts, and this is laid out in such a way as to collect all the necessary information. (See Chapter 4.)

These smaller charities may choose to prepare accounts under the accruals basis if they so wish, but if they do, then they must comply with the requirements of the accounting regulations and follow the recommendations of the SORP. Accruals accounts must consist of a SOFA and Balance Sheet. The SORP recommends that charities describe expenditure by activity and then give details of the breakdown into the normal expense-type headings in the notes to the accounts. However, under the accounting regulations, charities up to the £100,000 threshold may simplify the description of their expenditure in the SOFA. This means that they may use the normal expense-type headings they may have used in their old income and expenditure account, i.e. salaries, rent, rates, light, heat etc. In such cases the SOFA for many smaller charities will not be very different to the old income and expenditure account and this treatment is shown in the example in Chapter 5.

Charities Not Exceeding the £10,000 Threshold

Even smaller charities with neither gross income nor total expenditure exceeding £10,000 have to prepare accounts, but do not have to submit them to the Charity Commission unless requested to do so. In the case of unincorporated charities, these may be on the receipts and payments basis or accruals basis.

Exempt Charities

These are certain categories of charities which are exempt from registration with the Charity Commission and the sections of the Act relating to accounts and audit. In practice these charitable bodies are usually already subject to specific provisions relating to their accounts and audit under other regulatory bodies. Exempt charities are listed in Schedule 2 to the Act and include

◆ universities and colleges for higher education

◆ grant maintained schools

◆ museums and galleries

◆ Church Commissioners and bodies administered by them

◆ registered Industrial and Provident Societies and Friendly Societies

The accounts of these charities should follow the SORP, unless a more specific SORP applies, as would be the case for universities and housing associations.

Excepted Charities

These are certain categories of charities which do not have to register with the Charity Commission, although they may register if they wish. If they do register, then they must send in their annual report and accounts to the Charity Commission. However, if they are not registered, then they do not need to submit reports and accounts. The trustees still have a statutory duty to prepare annual accounts and they have to comply with other requirements, such as sending their accounts to a member of the public if requested to do so.

Charitable Companies

The relevant sections of the Act (sections 41-44) and accounting regulations 3 to 9 concerning the form and content of accounts do not apply to charitable companies. They are required to prepare accounts in the form prescribed by the Companies Acts and these accounts must show a true and fair view. In order to comply with the requirement to show a true and fair view, charitable companies will be expected to comply with the SORP. In practice, therefore, the format of their accounts should be very similar to that of unincorporated charities, although certain charitable companies may need to prepare a Summary Income and Expenditure Account as well as a Statement of Financial Activities. It does mean that charitable companies cannot opt for the receipts and payments basis; all accounts of companies must be prepared under the accruals basis and must be submitted to Companies House within ten months of the financial year end. (Note: there are penalties for the late submission of accounts to Companies House, which start at £100 for accounts up to three months late, rise to £250 for accounts filed three to six months late, £500 for accounts filed six to twelve months late, and £1,000 for accounts filed more than twelve months late).

Charity Commission Filing

Apart from the small charities up to the £10,000 threshold, all registered charities must submit their annual report and accounts within ten months of the financial year end to the Charity Commission, including charitable companies. In practice, the Charity Commission will be asking charities to submit both with the completed annual return for the year. The information required on the return will include extracts from the accounts, so it will in any case be easier to complete these all at the same time. Note that all charities will have to complete the annual return, including the very small charities.

Charity annual reports and accounts are available for public inspection at the Charity Commission offices.

In addition, members of the public may request a copy of the latest annual accounts of the charity and the charity must send them within two months. The charity may charge a reasonable fee for photocopying and postage.

Illustration

The audit and accounting requirements are effective from 1 March 1996. This means financial years commencing after that date. A charity which has a 31 March year end commences its first financial year affected by the regulations on 1 April 1996. The annual report and accounts drawn up for the year ended 31 March 1997 must comply with Part VI of the Act and the regulations.

The SORP represents best practice and therefore should be implemented as soon as possible. The charity should consider following the SORP for its financial year ending 31 March 1996.

Audit Requirements

Prior to the Charities Act 1993, unincorporated charities were not required by statute to have an audit. The trust deed or constitution may have set out an audit requirement, or it may have been a condition of certain grant funders. Section 43 of the Charities Act 1993 requires larger charities to have an audit for financial years commencing after 1 March 1996. So charities with a year end on 31 March will need to comply for the first time for the year ended 31 March 1997. Charities with a 31 December year end will have to comply for the first time for the year ended 31 December 1997. This part of the Charities Act 1993 does not apply to companies, as the audit regime for companies is already set out in the Companies Acts.

Larger charities are those with gross income or total expenditure exceeding £250,000 and they must be audited by a registered auditor. A registered auditor is an auditor who is qualified to undertake audits of companies and is regulated in his or her work. Firms of accountants are usually registered auditors. If a charity's gross income and total expenditure drops below the threshold of £250,000, it must continue to have a professional audit for a further two years.

Small Charities

Smaller charities i.e. those with gross income and total expenditure not exceeding £250,000 may instead have an "independent examination". This is a new type of external examination brought in by the Charities Act 1993 which may be undertaken by anyone with some experience of accounting, but who does not have to be a qualified accountant or auditor. Detailed guidance on the independent examination has been issued by the Charity Commission. Charities in this category may choose to have an audit, if the trustees think it is wise or if they have relatively complex affairs. It will be necessary to have an audit if the constitution requires it.

Very small charities i.e. those with gross income and total expenditure not exceeding £10,000 do not need to have a statutory audit or an independent examination, but they also must check their constitution.

Smaller and very small charities may need to contact the Charity Commission for advice on how the constitution may be amended so that they can take advantage of the reliefs from audit. In some cases, the governing document is old and the meaning of the word "audit" when the charity was established was not the same as the current usage, meaning an audit by a registered auditor. In that case, an independent examination may be sufficient under the terms of the governing document. This must be agreed by the Charity Commission and their approval to any change sought if necessary.

Example

A charity with gross income and total expenditure well below the threshold for audit each year wishes to opt for an independent examination. It wishes to do this as soon as possible. Its financial year ends on 31 December each year.

The charity needs to check its constitution or trust deed. If there is a clause in the constitution which requires an audit, then they will need to amend the clause. This will need to be done with the permission and approval of the Charity Commission.

Even then, the earliest year for which this charity will be able to have a statutory independent examination will be the year ending 31 December 1997.

Gross Income

For the purposes of assessing whether a charity exceeds the threshold for audit or not, the term "gross income" is defined as the total recorded income of the charity. The guidance accompanying annual returns from the Charity Commission states that this should not include the receipt of capital, the proceeds or profit from the sale of fixed assets or investments, loan repayments. It should include:

◆ donations, grants, gifts and legacies which do not constitute endowments

◆ covenanted income and the tax recoverable

◆ investment income (including interest receivable, dividends and rents)

◆ turnover from fees or trading activities in furtherance of the charity's objectives, membership subscriptions

◆ gross proceeds from fundraising other than for endowment

◆ other income, including amounts converted from expendable endowment to income

This definition should be followed to determine whether the audit threshold is exceeded or not, not the definition of incoming resources in the SORP.

Example

A charity with a financial year ending 31 March has gross income of £220,000 for 1998 and had gross income of £280,000 for the previous year. Do they need an audit?

Firstly, it is necessary to check the constitution or governing instrument to see whether that specifically requires an audit. Then check whether total expenditure is also below the £250,000 threshold. Because the charity exceeded the threshold in 1997 with gross income of £280,000, it will still have to have an audit in 1998 and 1999.

If the charity had gross income of £220,000 in 1997 and £280,000 in 1996, then the charity would not be over the threshold in the first year that the regulations apply. So there would be no need to have an audit, as the previous year would not count in those circumstances.

Total Expenditure

Total expenditure will include all the running costs of the organisation, all operating costs and depreciation (where accounts are prepared on the accruals basis). It will not include the making of a recoverable loan or the repayment of a loan. It also excludes expenditure on the purchase of fixed assets and investments.

Total expenditure needs to be checked as well as gross income when looking at the accounts to establish whether an audit is required. This may be particularly important when the gross income of a charity has been exceptionally high because of a particular fundraising drive in one year, which may have taken the charity over the threshold for audit. Then the gross income drops below the threshold for audit, but an audit is still required because the total expenditure is greater than gross income. An audit will then be required for a further two years.

Summary of Audit Requirements for Unincorporated Charities

Audit required if gross income or total expenditure exceeds £250,000

Audit required for further two years even if below threshold

Charities below £250,000 threshold may choose independent examination instead of audit

Charities with gross income or total expenditure below £10,000 do not have to have independent examination at all

Charities over £10,000 threshold must submit annual reports and accounts to Charity Commission within ten months of year end

---

Charitable Companies

Most of the accounting regulations and the provisions concerning the accounts and audit of charities do not affect charities which are also companies. These are covered by the Companies Act and are specifically excluded from the sections on accounts and audit in the 1993 Act. Until 11 August 1994, all companies were required to have an audit by a registered auditor. Now there are some exemptions for smaller companies.

Charitable companies with gross income below £250,000 and net assets of less than £1.4 million may opt to have a compilation report instead of an audit. (For non-charitable companies the threshold is £350,000 turnover.)

Companies with a gross income of up to £90,000 and a balance sheet total less than £1.4 million are not required to have an audit or a compilation report.

Additional Rules

There are some extra rules which companies must follow:

◆ All companies which are a subsidiary or have a subsidiary must have a full audit, regardless of turnover.

◆ All companies must prepare full accruals accounts and submit accounts to Companies House.

◆ 10% of the membership can request that an audit be performed, even if the company otherwise qualifies for the exemption.

◆ There is no rule about the audit requirement continuing as there is for unincorporated charities; the test is applied to the current year only.

Compilation Report

A compilation report is independent confirmation that the accounts have been properly prepared from the accounting records. It does not seek to confirm that the accounting records themselves are complete and accurate. An accountant will often prepare the accounts as well, although they could just review the accounts and compare them with the underlying records. The accountant ensures that the accounts are presented properly and disclose all the information required under the Companies Acts. He or she then reports under an "Accountant's Report" confirming that the accounts have been properly prepared.

Summary of Audit Requirements for Charitable Companies

Audit required if gross income more than £250,000, or net assets greater than £1.4m

All subsidiaries or parent companies must have audit

Compilation report required for charitable companies with gross income above £90,000 and up to £250,000

No external review at all for charitable companies with gross income below £90,000

All companies must prepare accounts in required form and submit them to Companies House within ten months of year end

Charitable companies must also submit their report and accounts to the Charity Commission within ten months of year end

Chapter 2

ANNUAL REPORTS

As well as annual accounts, registered charities (and excepted charities if requested) must prepare an annual report, which has to be submitted to the Charity Commission together with the accounts. This requirement applies to charitable companies as well as unincorporated charities, but they may incorporate the information required in the directors' report for Companies Act purposes into the annual report. Very small charities with gross income or total expenditure not exceeding £10,000 do not have to prepare and file an annual report. Charities with gross income below £100,000 may choose to prepare a simplified annual report, which includes only a brief summary of the activities and achievements of the charity in relation to its objects.

Summary of Requirements for Annual Report

Charities with gross income and total expenditure up to £10,000 do not have to prepare and file an annual report.

Charities above the £10,000 threshold but not exceeding £100,000 gross income may produce a simplified annual report, for filing with the accounts within ten months of the financial year end.

Charities above the £100,000 threshold must prepare a full report for filing with the accounts within ten months of the financial year end.

Requirements of the Accounting Regulations

The accounting regulations place the responsibility for preparing the annual report with the trustees. Even though the trustees may delegate the preparation of the annual report to individual trustees or members of staff, they are all responsible for it. The Statement of Recommended Practice for Charities (SORP) recommends that the annual report should be dated and signed by at least one duly authorised trustee on behalf of all trustees after approval at a trustees' meeting.

The accounting regulations require that the full annual report for charities will be a report on the financial year in relation to the charity's objects, to cover the following:

◆ a review of all activities

◆ all material transactions

◆ significant developments

◆ achievements in relation to the objects

◆ significant events since the year end

◆ future plans

The accounting regulations specifically require the following legal and administrative details to be included in the report:

◆ the name of the charity as it appears in the register and any other name by which it makes itself known

◆ the charity number and company number (if applicable)

◆ principal address (and registered office if a company)

◆ a description of the trusts of the charity

◆ names of the charity trustees (or 50 names including officers if there are more than 50 trustees)

◆ description of the organisational structure

◆ description of any assets held on behalf of another charity

Smaller charities (gross income not exceeding £100,000) do not have to provide information on the last two points.

The Charity Commission may give its permission for the names of trustees and the operational address of the charity to be omitted from the report. This will be in cases where such disclosure could lead to individuals being placed in personal danger. This clause is designed to cover the situations of women's refuges and other organisations where confidentiality is an important issue.

The information on legal and administrative details can be shown in the body of the report or it can be separated out onto a single sheet, as shown in the following example. The information in the example relates to a medium-sized charity, whose accounts appear in Chapter 6.

SORP Requirements

The SORP sets out the recommended contents of annual reports in more detail. Overall, the aim should be to give an account of the charity in a broad sense; financial statements can only give a limited picture of the activities of charities and the narrative explanations are important. The annual report should explain how the charity is meeting its objects and how it plans to do so in the future.

The headings in the annual report should be:

◆ Objects of charity and how it sets about its work

◆ Review of the development, activities and achievements of the charity during the year

◆ Review of the financial position of the charity and an explanation of the salient features of the accounts

◆ Explanations of relationships with any connected charities

The annual report is where volunteer help should be noted together with any other intangible income which is not valued and included in the accounts. Also statistics and information about the numbers of beneficiaries assisted in the year belong in the annual report. A reader of the annual report and accounts should be able to gain a rounded picture of the work of the charity.

Example Legal and Administrative Details

ELDERLY CONCERN CAMBERWICK
LEGAL AND ADMINISTRATIVE DETAILS
FOR THE YEAR ENDED 31 MARCH 1997

Name:	Elderly Concern Camberwick
Status:	Charity established as a company limited by guarantee (number 1098765) on 3 September 1983; registered with the Charity Commission number 896475
Principal Address:	The Highway Slippery Way Camberwick Wickshire
Charity Objects:	The charity is established to relieve poverty among elderly people in the area of Camberwick
Charity Trustees:	Tim Bloggins (Chairman) Adrian Waters (Vice-Chairman) Dilys Price (Secretary) Penny Farthing (Treasurer) Norman Price Trevor Winters Sylvia Pagett-Major Denise Hollins
Organisational Structure:	Elderly Concern Camberwick is an independent charity, although it is in contact with other similar charities, and in particular shares information with the network of charities under the Elderly Concern umbrella.
	The trustees are responsible for the overall management and control of the charity and receive reports from a sub-committee chaired by the treasurer on Finance and General Purposes.

Annual Report – SORP Checklist

Use this checklist as a reminder of the matters recommended in SORP for inclusion in the annual report. Not every point will apply to every charity and only matters which do apply need to be covered in the annual report.

The SORP is trying to clarify the type of points to be brought out in the annual report and the trustees should use their judgement as to what they put in and what they leave out. Headings may be omitted where there is nothing to report, but equally additional information should be put into the report to enable a reader of the report to understand the charity's position.

SORP Checklist	yes	n/a
1 Objects of charity and how it sets about its work		
1.1 Objects of charity as stated in its governing instrument	☐	☐
1.2 Summary of policies adopted in order to further objects	☐	☐
1.3 Any material changes in the policies since the last report and the reasons for those changes or a statement that there have been none	☐	☐
1.4 Description of the way in which the charity is organised e.g executive committee, sub-committees, branches	☐	☐
2 Review of the development, activities and achievements of the charity during the year		
2.1 General progress of the charity, and what it has been able to achieve during the year	☐	☐
2.2 Statistical information e.g. number of beneficiaries reached, how many times the charity's services have been called upon, the unit costs for services provided etc.	☐	☐
2.3 Important events which have occurred during the year, affecting the charity or the areas in which it works, and how the charity has responded to them	☐	☐
2.4 Services of unpaid volunteers or donations-in-kind (including facilities and services provided free to the charity) and other intangible income not evaluated or explained in the accounts	☐	☐
3 Review of the financial position of the charity, and an explanation of the salient features of the accounts		
3.1 How the charity's funds have been applied and the significance of all material movements in the Statement of Financial Activities	☐	☐
3.2 Purposes for which the charity's assets are being held and their estimated value if materially different from that shown in the accounts	☐	☐

3.3 The charity's financial position at the Balance Sheet ☐ ☐
     date in the context of its future plans and commitments,
     particularly with regard to on-going items of expenditure,
     projects not yet completed and obligations not yet met

3.4 Reasons for any changes in the accounting policies ☐ ☐
     of the charity and the effects of such changes, as
     disclosed in the accounts

3.5 Performance of any subsidiary and associated ☐ ☐
     undertakings whose results are included in
     the consolidated accounts of the charity or in
     the notes to the charity accounts

3.6 Effects on present and future accounts of any ☐ ☐
     revaluations of fixed assets made during the period,
     other than of investments

3.7 The extent to which the charity may be financially ☐ ☐
     dependent upon the support of any individuals,
     corporations, or classes of donors known to play
     a key role in its affairs

3.8 The nature of any important events affecting the ☐ ☐
     charity which have occurred between the date
     of the Balance Sheet and the date on which the
     Annual Report is signed

3.9 Where the charity was set up to undertake a ☐ ☐
     specific project, the progress of that project. This
     part of the review should give cumulative figures
     of funding and expenditure on the project to date,
     with estimates of the additional costs and period
     of time required to complete

3.10 That any investments held by the charity have been ☐ ☐
      acquired in accordance with the powers available
      to the trustees

3.11 On a fund-by-fund basis, confirmation or otherwise ☐ ☐
      that the charity's assets are available and adequate
      to fulfil the obligations of the charity, with specific
      reference to:

  • any likely delays or shortfalls in realising those ☐ ☐
    assets into cash

  • any commitments or guarantees required to ☐ ☐
    be disclosed

  • the position resulting from revaluations of fixed ☐ ☐
    assets shown in the Balance Sheet

4 Explanations of relationships with any ☐ ☐
connected charities

Example Annual Report

The following example is the actual annual report of the charity Barnardo's for the year ended 31 March 1995. This example covers all the main points recommended in the SORP. Obviously, this is a large charity, but it does demonstrate how the recommendations can be applied in practice.

BARNARDO'S
Annual Report of the Council

The Council submits the Report and Accounts for the year ended 31 March 1995

Basis and values

Barnardo's is a charity whose inspiration and values derive from the Christian faith. These values, enriched and shared by many people of other faiths and philosophies, provide the basis of our work with children and young people, their families and communities.

Barnardo's wishes to: -

- respect the unique worth of every person
- encourage people to fulfil their potential
- work with hope
- exercise responsible stewardship

Objects

The objects of Barnardo's as defined by the Memorandum of Association are:

(i)   the relief and assistance of children and young people in need

(ii) the promotion of the education of children and young people

(iii) the promotion among children and young people of the knowledge of the Christian faith or the faith in which they were brought up

(iv) the relief of the poor, sick, handicapped and aged

Current focus

The current focus of Barnardo's work is to: -

- provide social welfare services for the benefit of children and young people most in need of them
- promote good practice and developments in services
- influence social welfare policy
- raise awareness of and encourage good child care

These purposes are pursued by responding to children, young people and families who:-

- are experiencing significant disadvantage and where poverty is a powerful determinant
- have significant disability
- are experiencing isolation, especially those living at the margins of society
- are experiencing discrimination

Barnardo's currently manages more than 200 projects and schemes which cover five main areas of work:-

1. Families with young children

This work includes centres for young children and their families, incorporating a variety of day care programmes, including day fostering, playgroups, toy libraries, family counselling, development of parenting skills and advice on child development. Work was also undertaken with travelling families and family assessment work for Local Authorities. In 1994/95 5,531 children together with their families were assisted (1993/94 – 4,721).

2. Children and young people with disabilities

Barnardo's provides a range of residential care and other support services to families caring at home for a young person with a disability or to families with other special needs. The services include advice, counselling, conciliation, family therapy, holiday play schemes, sitting services, short term respite care, youth training and self help initiatives. The number of people assisted was 6,395 in 1994/95 (1993/94 – 6,397).

3. Children needing families

Fostering, adoption and counselling work aided 2,181 (1993/94 – 1,341) children and young people with special needs during the year. There were 56 adoption orders in 1994/95 (1993/94 – 67).

4. Disadvantaged young people

This covers projects which help teenagers living alone in the community, diverting young people from custody, youth training schemes, preventative work among adolescents, residential and after care services. This also includes church and community work and work with adolescents involved with drug and solvent abuse. Some 11,345 young people benefited in 1994/95 (1993/94 – 10,020).

5. Children and young people with educational needs

Residential and non-residential schools and centres provided services in 1994/95 to 1,141 (1993/94 – 1,028) children and young people, who have emotional/behavioural difficulties or physical or learning disabilities.

Adult services

During the last 25 years Barnardo's has established a series of projects which provide residential care for children with learning disabilities. The residents of some of these projects have now grown into adulthood, and during 1994/95 several of these projects were transferred to United Response, a charity specialising in the provision of services for adults with learning disabilities or mental health problems. A number of other projects will transfer during the next two years.

Agenda for action

In February 1991 Barnardo's launched an Agenda for Action to develop new work in three priority areas – sexual abuse, homelessness and HIV/AIDS. By March 1995 a total of 103 proposals had been approved, the majority of which are extensions to existing projects, rather than entirely new ventures. During 1994/95 expenditure amounted to £2.0 million. Barnardo's aims to develop and implement further proposals in these three areas and also to continue to respond to needs in other areas. It is anticipated that this will lead to a steady growth in the volume of services.

Corporate governance

Barnardo's is a company limited by guarantee and a registered charity. Its governing instrument is the Memorandum and Articles of Association as amended and adopted by special resolution passed on 18 October 1994. Its governing body is a Council whose members are elected by the Members of Association. As at July 1995 the Council comprises 25 members. The Council meets five times during the year, it is assisted by a number of committees: the main Committee of Council is the Executive/Finance Committee which comprises 12 members of Council and meets monthly; this Committee oversees the implementation of Council's policies, proposes courses of action to the Council and considers recommendations from the Senior Director and the three National Directors.

Other committees are:

- Audit Committee
- Investment Committee
- Trading Committee
- Membership of Association and New Members of Council Committee
- Adoption Sub-Committee

All Council members have access to the advice and services of the Company Secretary.

The salaries of the Senior Director and the three National Directors are determined by Council upon their appointment and by periodic review; they receive cost of living increases on an annual basis.

Organisation

Responsibility for operational activities is allocated to three departments, Child Care, Appeals and Corporate Services. Child Care is divided geographically into eight divisions operating from Belfast, Birmingham, Cardiff, Edinburgh, Leeds, Liverpool, London and Newcastle. The Appeals Department operates from the Head Office in Barkingside and also from a number of regional offices. The Corporate Services Department, which includes the Finance, Personnel, Properties and Publicity functions, is also based at Head Office and provides support services to both Child Care and Appeals.

Barnardo's also provides significant financial support by way of grant aid for work undertaken by Barnardo's Republic of Ireland, an associated charity. Barnardo's Australia and Barnardo's New Zealand are locally registered charities, raise funds for use in their own countries and are managed by local Committees of Management; during 1994/95 they became legally independent. Accordingly the financial transactions of these associated charities are not included in the accompanying accounts.

Finance

Revised Statement of Recommended Practice on Accounting by Charities (SORP 2)

In February 1995, a revised draft of the Statement of Recommended Practice No 2 on Accounting by Charities was published. Council welcomes the objective of improving the quality of financial reporting by charities and has adopted, with some minor exceptions, the recommendations of the revised SORP 2.

The principal change is the introduction of a Statement of Financial Activities in place of the Consolidated Income and Expenditure Account. This gives a clearer statement of the resources receivable and expended by the charity during the year.

Review of transactions and financial position

The balance sheet on page 11 indicates that at 31 March 1995 the total funds of the charity were £174 million. This was represented by Tangible Fixed Assets of £72.4 million, Investments of £85.5 million and Net Current Assets of £16.1 million. Unrestricted funds of £95.5 million represents the reserves available to the organisation to fulfil its many existing commitments over the long-term and also to finance the growth in activity envisaged in future plans.

The Council regularly reviews the reserve levels in the light of planned activities, and for 1994/95 approved the use of part of the reserves for the establishment of new projects.

Accordingly, the Statement of Financial Activities on page 10 indicates that total resources expended for the year ended 31 March 1995 was £84.6 million. This exceeded the total income generated of £79.1 million. The planned deficit of £5.4 million was financed primarily by the sale of investments. Unrealised losses on investments of £7.1 million were recognised during the year. In common with other organisations, Barnardo's investment portfolio suffered reductions in its value as a result of stock market weaknesses, particularly in the UK. This contrasted with significant increases in value in preceding years.

Trading activities

The results of Barnardo's subsidiary companies are summarised in Note 2 of the accounts. Barnardo Publications suffered a second year of difficult trading; a new management team has been installed and the Directors of the company; with the approval of the Trustees, have agreed a restructuring plan designed to restore the business to its former levels of profitability.

Net income generated by the subsidiaries was £1.8 million. In addition, Barnardo's shops produced a surplus of £2.8 million from the sale of donated goods.

Valuation of land and buildings

Although some properties would individually realise sums considerably in excess of their book value, others have been purpose-built or specially adapted for a particular use and might not realise their cost. It is therefore not practical to estimate the difference between market value and book value and in view of the fact that the properties are occupied for charitable purposes, Council does not consider the expense of an independent valuation justified.

Irrecoverable VAT

During the year ended 31 March 1995 the charity incurred irrecoverable VAT in excess of £2 million.

Auditors

In accordance with Section 384 of the Companies Act 1985 resolutions proposing the re-appointment of Ernst & Young as auditors of the Company and to authorise Council to fix their remuneration, will be put to the Members at the Annual General Meeting.

Members of Council

A list of Members of Council who have served during the year and composition of the Executive/Finance Committee appears on page 23.

Members retiring by rotation in accordance with Article 42 are: Mrs S E Bagot, Mr T R Lawson, Miss J A Lewis-Jones, Mr C H Martin and Mrs K Murray.

The following Members retire in accordance with Article 43: Professor N A Jepson and Dr J Robins.

All the aforementioned Members being eligible offer themselves for re-election. The following members retire in accordance with Article 43 and are ineligible for re-election, having reached the age of 75: Mrs M R O Patey, Mr J K Rice-Oxley. During the year Mr B C Johnston and Mrs M W Nicol resigned. Council wishes to record its appreciation of the unstinting service given by all four members to Barnardo's.

Planning, consultation and communication

The Management structure of Barnardo's is such that all operational aspects of child care work are controlled by Divisional Directors working closely with overall objectives and policy guidelines determined by Council. Divisional Directors in consultation with their staff are responsible for deciding on priorities in selecting new child care work and on recommending start-up and closure of all the projects under their control. Senior Appeals Managers in consultation with their staff are responsible for the planning and execution of all fundraising operations.

Local and central management involve staff at all levels in forward planning and the agreement of prime objectives. Professional child care issues are discussed at national and local training events. There are regular meetings involving all the staff in a particular area, within a specialism or having a common interest in a specific subject. Staff views are sought where changes in conditions of service are contemplated other than matters (including salary scales) settled by agreements in the public sector.

Staff contribute to and receive regular Barnardo's News and other publications featuring topical staff news and articles on aspects of Barnardo's activities. Information bulletins are also produced as required to inform staff of important development and changes.

Equal opportunities

Barnardo's is committed to ensuring equality of opportunity for its staff and for the children, young people and families with whom it works in partnership. It is fundamental to the charity's high standards of child care work.

Barnardo's believes that selection and promotion should be based solely on ability to meet the requirements of the post. The aim is to remove discrimination, to provide equal access to jobs and training and to ensure that all staff enjoy fully the benefits of working for the organisation.

In particular Barnardo's is committed to preventing discrimination on the grounds of sex/gender, marital status, race, sexual orientation, religion or disability.

However, in pursuit of the Equal Opportunity Policy, occasional use is made of the positive action clauses in present legislation. Guardianship of the Basis and Values rests with the National Directors who have to be committed Christians.

Special acknowledgements

Council wishes to record its appreciation of the generosity of the many friends of Barnardo's for their donations and bequests and to the thousands of volunteers who give so unstintingly of their time. Barnardo's has also benefited from help received from companies, organisations, local authorities and individuals in the form of gifts in kind, free loans of property, preferential rent and part-relief from rates. By the terms of the gift the following special acknowledgements are made:

Grant	Children in Need £350,000, being the final instalment of a total grant of £956,000 in support of Barnardo's HIV/AIDS programme.
Discretionary	Discretionary payment received from the Executors of the Lord Austin Trust – general award – £2,268.
Discretionary	Discretionary payment received from the Executors of the Tom Parrington Charity for Accrington BHL – £75
Income	Income from the "Bettine Ward Memorial Trust Fund" for adventure training – £446
Grants	Albert Reckitt Charitable Trust – £500

By Order of the Council
Gordon Travis
Company Secretary
18 July 1995

Example for a Medium-sized Charity

An example is given below to show how the annual report can be incorporated into the directors' report for a charitable company. The example links to the legal and administrative details given earlier in this chapter. The content relates to the the accounts in Chapter 6 and together with the auditor's report in Chapter 8, this would form the financial statements for this organisation. Chapters 4 and 5 includes examples of the trustees' report for small unincorporated charities.

ELDERLY CONCERN CAMBERWICK
Director's Report
for the year ended 31 March 1997

The directors present their report and the audited financial statements for the year ended 31 March 1997

Activities and Review

The company is a charity and exists to relieve poverty amongst the elderly of Camberwick. To achieve this object, the charity operates a number of projects.

Advice and Advocacy

This project is based at the central office and provides help and advice to elderly people. The main type of advice concerns their entitlement to benefits and social services. Several information leaflets have been produced and these are now available in five languages in addition to English. Individual advice is provided at drop-in times and also by special appointment. This service also assists carers who need advice. As a result of the advice service, a carers support group has been set up on the Walberswick Green Estate.

The project is funded by the Borough of Camberwick and employs four part-time staff. The mainstay of the service are the many volunteers who provide advice and distribute information leaflets. In 1996/97 over 1,000 volunteer hours were donated and 1,200 people were assisted. The receipt of a donation from the Camberwick Charitable Trust has enabled us to buy a new computer and database software, which will be used to organise information and make it more easily accessible.

Domiciliary Care

The work of the charity of providing elderly people with assistance in their own homes continued to expand during 1996/97. At the beginning of the year, we had set a target to reach 50 new housebound elderly to bring the number receiving this service on a regular basis up to 250. Whilst there has been no problem finding the people in need of the service, it has been difficult to find domiciliary care assistants. Consequently, we did not achieve our target in terms of providing a regular service to the new people. This should be achieved within the near future, and funds are available within restricted funds for us to complete this aspect of the service.

We also wanted to find out whether the service did meet the needs of elderly people. To this end, 20 volunteers from the local TEC undertook a survey on our behalf. The results of this are still being processed, but should give us valuable information for planning future services.

We work in close co-operation with Wickshire County Council Social Services department in operating this project. We are grateful for their support and funding. By 1998, it is planned that this service will transfer to a contract, the terms of which will be agreed in the course of this coming year.

Luncheon Club

The contract with Wickshire County Council to run a luncheon club for elderly people in the Camberwick area continues to run successfully. On average about 75 people use the club each day, which is an increase of 50% compared to the attendance when it was run by the Social Services Department. The club still operates from the same premises owned by the County Council, which were given a complete facelift in 1996. Now the bright and cheerful atmosphere hosts all sorts of activities as well as the actual lunch each day. These activities would not be possible without the enormous efforts of our volunteers. We are also grateful to the staff at Wick Dial-A-Ride service, who transport so many of our clients.

Directors and Their Interests

Those who served as directors and trustees during the year and up to the date of this report were as follows:

> Jim Higgins (resigned 24 September 1996)
> Angus Farthing (resigned 11 November 1996)
> Tim Bloggins
> Adrian Waters
> Dilys Price
> Penny Farthing
> Norman Price
> Trevor Winters
> Silvia Pagett-Major (appointed 22 October 1996)
> Denise Hollins (appointed 14 April 1997)

No director has any beneficial interest in the company. All directors are members of the company and guarantee to contribute £1 in the event of a winding up. The number of guarantees at 31 March 1997 was 8 (1996 – 8).

Directors' Responsibilities

Company law requires the directors, who are also the charity trustees, to prepare financial statements for each financial year which give a true and fair view of the state of the affairs of the company and of the surplus or deficit of the company for that period. In preparing those financial statements, the directors are required to:

- select suitable accounting policies and then apply them consistently;
- make judgements and estimates that are reasonable and prudent;
- state whether applicable accounting standards have been followed, subject to any material departures disclosed and explained in the financial statements;
- prepare the financial statements on the going concern basis unless it is inappropriate to assume that the company will continue on that basis.

Presentation of Annual Reports

The trustees' annual report does not have to be the same document as the expensively printed annual review produced by many charities. Indeed, its purpose may be quite different. The trustees' annual report has to include specific information relating to the financial statements. For the purpose of filing with the Charity Commissioners it will be attached to the full financial statements, together with the auditor's report. They are designed to be read together. Charities may wish to produce a different document for fundraising or public relations.

If a charity does consider producing a "glossy" annual report or annual review, then the trustees need to consider whether they wish to include financial information in it. Basically, there are three options:

◆ omit financial information

◆ include the full financial statements

◆ include summarised accounts

Omit Financial Information

If no accounts or summarised accounts are included in the annual review, then there are no specific rules to follow. The information in the annual review must be accurate and should not mislead anyone and this would obviously include any financial information. Any claims which relate to the financial health or results of the charity must of course be justifiable. So for example a charity should not claim that it has very low reserves when in fact these are 125% of the annual expenditure budget unless the operational requirements of its work dictate a much higher level than this.

There is no requirement for the auditors to review this document before it is circulated and it does not have to be sent to the Charity Commission. It is additional to the trustees' annual report, which should have accompanied the accounts.

Include Full Financial Statements

The second option would be to include the full financial statements in the annual review. This would mean that the narrative would be the trustees' annual report and that all the accounts, including the notes to the accounts, have to be reproduced in full. The full auditors' report should be included; audit practice dictates that the auditors' report may only be reproduced if it is printed in full and only when the full accounts are also printed.

This obviously has significant cost implications, but it may be necessary or appropriate for organisations with a large membership base. All members of a company must be sent a copy of the full accounts after approval by the directors, but before the Annual General Meeting. Similar rules may exist in unincorporated charities, which will usually be spelt out in the constitution.

Summarised Accounts

The third option is to produce a printed annual review which incorporates summarised financial information. If this option is chosen, then the SORP gives some very specific guidelines on how the summarised accounts should be presented. The summarised accounts should be a fair and accurate summary of the full accounts. The full annual report and accounts should always be produced in addition to any summary and should be available to anyone requesting them. Summarised accounts should contain information relating to both the Statement of Financial Activities and the Balance Sheet.

Summarised accounts should be accompanied by a statement, signed on behalf of the trustees, that they are a summary of information extracted from the annual accounts.

They must also contain a warning statement, alerting readers to the fact that summarised accounts may not contain sufficient information for a full understanding of the charity's affairs. It should also state when the annual accounts were approved and whether the accounts have been submitted to the Charity Commission and (for companies only) Companies House.

The statement should say whether the accounts have been audited or examined, and whether any opinion given on the accounts was qualified or not. If the report was qualified, then an explanation of the qualification may be necessary. It will only be appropriate to publish the full audit report if the full accounts are also published with it.

Example Statement with Summarised Accounts

These summarised accounts are a summary of information extracted from the audited annual accounts, on which the auditors' opinion was unqualified. The full report and accounts were approved by the trustees on 13 September 1997 and have been submitted to the Charity Commission and the Registrar of Companies. These summarised accounts may not contain sufficient information to allow for a full understanding of the financial affairs of the charity. For further information the full accounts, the auditor's report on those accounts and the Trustees' Annual Report should be consulted. Copies of these may be obtained from the Secretary at The Works, Islington High Street, London, N1.

Signed on behalf of the Trustees

Jo Bloggs

20 September 1997

In addition to the warning statement by the trustees, the auditor has to give an opinion as to whether the summarised accounts are consistent with the full accounts.

Example Auditors' Statement with Summarised Accounts

As auditors to the charity, we have reviewed the summarised accounts above and consider that they are consistent with the full accounts, on which we gave our opinion.

Signed

....

Auditors

....

Date

Statement of Auditing Standard

Under an auditing standard, auditors are also required to review any written reports published with financial statements. This includes the trustees' annual report issued with the full audited accounts, but may also include the glossy annual review published by some charities. Auditors need to check that there is no inconsistency between the financial statements and the narrative report. If they find any problems, then this would be brought to the attention of the management and trustees in the first instance. In the rare situation where the error is not rectified, then the auditors would have to take the further step of circulating a statement to all possible readers of the report, drawing their attention to the inconsistency.

Chapter 3

OVERVIEW OF BEST PRACTICE

The first version of the Statement of Recommended Practice for Charities (SORP) was introduced in May 1988, but was only implemented very slowly. It was criticised for being too flexible and giving charities options, instead of prescribing suitable treatments for certain transactions. It has also become out of date on certain matters as these have been dealt with in accounting standards.

A revised SORP was drawn up by a committee drawn together by the Charity Commission and published as an Exposure Draft on 17 March 1993. It was always intended that the SORP would be consistent with the accounting regulations of the Charities Act 1993 and so the various bodies worked together and a further revised draft of the charities SORP was issued in February 1995. With a few further changes the final version was issued in October 1995 at the same time as the accounting regulations.

The accounting regulations have statutory force as they implement Part VI of the Charities Act 1993, but the provisions relating to the form and content of the accounts only apply to unincorporated charities. The accounting regulations are relatively short, however, and do not go into detail. The SORP covers the same points, but also expands on the accounting regulations. Broadly, a charity may be confident that it is complying with the accounting regulations if it is following the SORP.

The charities SORP applies to all charities, other than specialised charities such as registered housing associations and universities, which have their own SORPs. So this includes charitable companies, trusts, excepted charities, charitable Industrial and Provident Societies and many other exempt charities. Whilst it is not mandatory, trustees should explain their reasons if they do not follow recommended practice and auditors should draw attention to the matter in their audit report if they do not agree that the departure from the recommended practice is fully explained and justified. The Charity Commissioners state in a foreword to the SORP:

> "The Commissioners expect the accounts of charities and their accounting practices to comply fully with this or any other applicable SORP. In so far as a charity diverges from the SORP in material respects, the charity's accounts should identify any divergence clearly and provide a full explanation. Where no explanation is given or the explanation is unsatisfactory, the Commission will decide whether or not to raise the matter with the charity concerned and, if circumstances warrant it, institute an inquiry."

The statutory requirement for accounts to show a true and fair view is a strong imperative for charities to follow the SORP, even though it is not itself mandatory.

SORP – THE MAIN POINTS

Statement of Financial Activities

A new financial statement has been introduced into charity accounting called the Statement of Financial Activities (SOFA), which, for most charities, replaces the income and expenditure account. The SOFA introduces some important changes in the basic concepts underlying accounts. The income and expenditure account was based on the profit and loss account, which aims to measure the profitability of commercial enterprises. The SORP is asserting that this is generally unsuitable for charities, because they are "not-for-profit" bodies. The surplus or deficit on an income and expenditure account can be very misleading, as often a surplus may represent funds which are committed, but the normal accounting rules do not allow charities to show the committed expenditure. Alternatively, a deficit for the year may be due to a responsible management committee ensuring that they use up reserves they have built up previously. So the SOFA tries to move away from surplus and deficit and the terms do not appear at all. Instead the emphasis is on showing all incoming resources, all expenditure and all fund movements. The SOFA has to show the fund balances brought forward as well as the result for the year, and then the fund balances at the end of the year.

Capital or Endowment Property

One of the most significant changes is the inclusion of new capital resources as an incoming resource. So, for example, the initial gift of a building or sum of money which is given under terms which make it a permanent endowment will be included in the SOFA. It cannot be described as income, because that would be contradictory, but it is part of the charity's incoming resources. In the SORP, the incoming resources are all the receipts and funds due to the charity for the period. This is revolutionary in accounting terms, because a basic accounting concept is that capital and revenue are dealt with separately in the accounts.

Traditionally, capital receipts go direct to the balance sheet, as for example when a company raises capital by issuing shares. The argument behind the change for charities is, of course, that they are not commercial entities and therefore the split between capital and income does not have the same meaning. The identification of capital is still important for a charity, because that determines what it may or may not do with particular assets. A charity may not dispose of the assets it has received as a permanent endowment, but should keep them and produce income or other benefit from them, which it should use for the objects of the charity. For a commercial entity, however, the capital is held by shareholders, who own the company and expect a return on their shares. This is totally different; no-one "owns" a charity. A permanent endowment is an outright gift and the original owner of the property may not retain any beneficial interest in the property.

The problem the SORP seeks to address is the practice of effectively understating their income by keeping one-off gifts (not necessarily the same as endowments) off the income and expenditure account. As an example of this, it was relatively common practice for charities to have a "legacy equalisation account". Legacies received during the year would be credited to this balance sheet account, not to income. Then the charity would release a certain amount of income from the legacy equalisation account to the income and expenditure account each year. The idea was to "annualise" a lump sum receipt and many charities operated a consistent policy with stated periods over which they would equalise legacies received. Where this was disclosed properly, it was not necessarily a bad accounting policy, but it did lead to discrepancies between charities. Sometimes, however, there was no consistent policy, and the charity transferred an amount to balance up the expenditure for the year. There are also many examples of charities who extended this method of accounting to all sorts of income, including appeals and ordinary fundraised income. These practices were somewhat harder to justify.

These practices made it very difficult for readers of accounts to see what the total incoming resources of charities was; bits of income were in any number of notes to the accounts explaining the movement on balance sheet reserves. The SORP requires all incoming resources to be shown in the SOFA.

If the charity has incoming resources on endowment funds, then it will have to prepare an income and expenditure account in addition to the SOFA. This can take a very simplified form, but would exclude the incoming capital. Financial Reporting Standard 3 (FRS 3) requires a revenue account to show the operating surplus or deficit, as does company legislation. The examples in Chapter 6 and Chapter 7 demonstrate the summary income and expenditure account layout. Further details about summary income and expenditure accounts are given at the end of this chapter.

Netting Off

Following on from the above, it is also logical that the SORP has banned the "netting off" of income and expenditure. This was also common practice amongst charities, especially in relation to fundraising activities. It meant that the profit from the fundraising activity was shown, but the gross income and associated expenditure was not necessarily disclosed. The SORP requires the gross income to be shown under an appropriate heading under incoming resources and the associated expenditure under fundraising and publicity costs, or whatever the appropriate heading is. The principle applies to all incoming resources and expenditure, not just fundraising activities. The aim is to ensure that the gross incoming resources of the charity are shown in full and that the costs are shown in full. Charities may give further information in the notes or the annual report if they wish, for example to show the net proceeds from fundraising activities.

Fund Accounting

Charity accounts will be different from those of commercial entities in another important way. The accounts will identify different types of funds according to the terms under which they were given to the charity.

Fund Accounting

The acconts must deal with the three major types of funds:

Capital funds............... funds to be retained by the charity (endowment)

Restricted funds .... income funds for spending on specific purposes

Unrestricted funds ..... income funds for spending in furtherance of the charity's stated objects

These distinctions are drawn to recognise the different legal restrictions over what a charity may do with funds it receives. There is an overriding requirement that the charity must apply all funds in furtherance of the stated charitable objects, but sometimes charities receive funds as special trusts. The funds structure of charities will be:

Restricted	**Unrestricted**
Permanent Endowment Funds	Designated Funds
Expendable Endowment Funds	General Funds
Restricted Income Funds	

Permanent Endowment Funds are funds which have been given to a charity to be held as capital with no power to convert the funds to income. These may be cash or other assets. Although the capital must be retained for the benefit of the charity, any investment income will be available for application unless otherwise specified by the terms of the trust.

Expendable Endowment Funds are funds which have been given to a charity to be held as capital, where the trustees do have a discretionary power of conversion into income. They remain capital in nature until so converted.

Restricted Funds are funds subject to special trusts specified by the donor. This might be because it was a public appeal for a specific purpose, grants or donations. It may also include land, buildings or other assets donated to a charity. Restricted funds may be restricted income funds, which are expendable at the discretion of the trustees in furtherance of some particular aspect of the objects of the charity. Or they may be capital funds, where the assets are required to be invested, or retained for actual use, rather than expended. Restricted capital funds are termed endowment funds as described above and accounted for separately. Restricted income funds may be grouped together for presentation in the SOFA, but detailed records will need to be kept of each fund. The trustees will be in breach of trust if they use restricted income other than for the specified purpose. Investment income arising from a restricted fund must be added to the fund.

Unrestricted Funds are funds available for the purposes of the charity, to be spent as the trustees see fit within the stated objects of the charity. The trustees are free to set priorities and decide how and when to spend the funds.

Designated Funds are unrestricted funds which have been earmarked for a particular purpose by the trustees. The notes to the accounts should explain the purpose of designated funds.

General Funds are unrestricted funds which have not been earmarked and may be used generally to further the charity's objects.

Incoming Resources and Application of Resources

Charities are required to account for incoming resources and the application of those resources by fund. The SOFA will usually be in a columnar format, so that the movement on each type of fund is shown as well as the overall total. The main funds to be shown are capital, restricted and unrestricted, with further detail in notes to analyse these funds further into their components if necessary. Many charities do not have all the types of funds and it is not necessary to show columns for funds unless they apply to your charity. Indeed, some charities only have unrestricted income and therefore the SOFA will not look much different in layout to an old income and expenditure account. They merely need to explain in a note that all income is unrestricted.

Fund accounting applies to balance sheets as well and the balances on each fund must be shown on the balance sheet. Assets and liabilities must be identified to each fund and this can be done on the face of the balance sheet in a columnar form like the SOFA, or in a note to the accounts.

Gains and Losses

The general principle is that gains and losses belong to the fund to which the assets belong. However, income arising from the investment of assets in an endowment fund may be applied to the charity's general purposes unless the terms of the trusts specifically state otherwise. Investment income, such as interest earned on restricted income funds placed in a deposit account, is part of the income to the restricted funds, although the terms of the restricted fund may allow income arising to be used for general purposes. It is important therefore to check the terms of the particular fund. It may be necessary to apportion deposit interest if you have a mixture of restricted and unrestricted funds in one deposit account. Providing there is adequate separation of funds in the accounting records, this would be acceptable, unless the funds were very significant and held for a long period, in which case a separate bank deposit account may be advisable.

Thus, a profit made on the disposal of some fixed assets which were part of a restricted fund will be added to the restricted fund (or a loss taken away). For example, the organisation's minibus may be written off for insurance purposes after a crash; the insurance proceeds are greater than the net book value of the minibus, so in accounting terms there is a profit on disposal. If the minibus is part of the restricted funds of the charity because it was originally purchased with funds donated specifically for that purpose, then the profit on disposal has to be shown in the restricted funds.

Transfers Between Funds

There will be occasions where a transfer is necessary between funds. Some transfers are quite straightforward and just have to be disclosed and explained properly. For example, a transfer from the general funds to the designated funds is not technically a transfer, but may be disclosed. Both general and designated funds are part of unrestricted funds, and the trustees may move funds around between these two sub-categories if they wish.

There will be occasions where it is necessary to move funds from unrestricted to restricted, and this does not present too many problems either. For example, a charity may have been fundraising specifically to purchase new equipment for a nursery. The income has been put into restricted funds, but there is a shortfall the charity wishes to make up from its unrestricted funds. It will be appropriate to transfer the funds from unrestricted to restricted. The equipment purchased will then all belong to restricted funds. This approach is preferable to splitting fixed assets into part restricted and part unrestricted.

More difficult is a transfer from restricted to unrestricted funds. The situation could arise where a charity has a balance on a restricted fund, which cannot be applied to the specified purpose. It may be that the purpose has already been met, that more money was received than was needed for the purpose, that the purpose no longer exists, or various other reasons. Because the funds are held on special trust, the charity may have to pay the funds back to the donors, or the donors may be asked if they will allow the funds to be used for the general purposes of the charity. If neither of these solutions are possible, then the charity needs to ask the Charity Commission to make a scheme (an amendment of the special trust) to allow them to transfer the funds to unrestricted funds.

Each kind of transfer between funds should be shown separately, rather than all lumped together, which would mean netting off the transfers. If necessary, further explanation of the reasons for the transfers should be given in the notes to the accounts.

Expenditure Classification

The SORP introduces new headings which should be used for expenditure in the SOFA. The main headings are:

Direct Charitable Expenditure – sub-divided into:

Grants payable

Expenditure on activities

Support costs

Other Expenditure – sub-divided into:

Fundraising and publicity costs

Management and administration of the charity

Expenditure should be classified by "function" not by its "natural" classification. The function refers to the activities of the charity, so to what purpose the money was spent. For example, a charity which provides services to the elderly might have three main activities and beneath the heading Direct Charitable Expenditure, it would group expenditure under sub-headings such as:

Luncheon Club

Home Visiting

Advice and Counselling Service

The SORP obviously cannot spell out what those headings ought to be for each charity, but each charity needs to think about how it would describe its activities.

The natural classification is the old style list of expenditure headings such as salaries, rent, rates, light, heat, insurance, etc. This information needs to be given as well in the notes to the accounts, so that a reader may understand how the amount spent on a particular activity is made up. (Under the accounting regulations, small charities, i.e. gross income up to £100,000, may choose to retain the natural classification in the SOFA rather than the functional classification.)

Fundraising is another "function" and so is the management and administration of the charity. These are defined below.

Expenditure Analysis

Clearly, charities will have to analyse expenditure between different headings to achieve the functional classification. This will have implications for the way in which their bookkeeping is undertaken. Most straightforward bookkeeping systems analyse expenditure by its natural classification, whereas some direct costs will need to be identified to activities or projects as well. Another dimension is needed for the bookkeeping and this can be time-consuming and difficult for manual systems. A cost-centre approach will be a good basis for producing the information required for the SOFA. Computerised systems do usually have some form of cost centre analysis as well as the natural analysis, but a simple system may not have the facility to do all the apportionment which may be necessary. Manual or spreadsheet analysis at the year end may be quite adequate. Some costs will have to be apportioned on an estimated basis anyway. A percentage of staff time and overheads may need to be apportioned to a particular activity or project heading. The basis should be applied consistently and auditors may require some evidence to demonstrate that the basis is fair. It helps to think about the basis and appropriate percentages when drawing up budgets, as it depends greatly on how the organisation operates and is managed.

When allocating and apportioning expenditure, it is useful to bear in mind the definitions of the various expenditure categories.

Direct Charitable Expenditure comprises all expenditure directly relating to the objects of the charity. It should include grants payable and the direct cost of charitable activities and projects (e.g. salaries, office, communications and other costs identifiable as an integral part of the cost of carrying out those charitable activities or projects), as well as depreciation and loss on disposal of fixed assets where these are used wholly or mainly for direct charitable activities. The SOFA should show some headings under the category of direct charitable expenditure as appropriate to describe the activities of the charity.

Support Costs are part of the direct charitable expenditure and may be the management of projects from a central office. Support costs may be omitted as a heading if these costs are absorbed as part of the direct project expenditure.

Fundraising and Publicity Costs are the costs of obtaining funds for the charity's work, such as advertising, direct mail, staff time, agent's fees. Fundraising costs should not be netted off against income.

Management and Administration Costs of the charity are the costs incurred in the management of the charity's assets, organisational administration and statutory requirements. For example, the cost of audit and trustees' meetings would fall into this category. Charities should first identify costs to direct charitable and fundraising cost categories. Costs which cannot be justifiably charged to another category must be put into management and administration.

The expenditure analysis will also have to split expenditure between funds. Usually the split will be between restricted income funds and unrestricted income funds. Occasionally, expenditure will need to be analysed to capital funds in certain circumstances. Generally, management and administrative costs will properly fall under unrestricted expenditure. It will be possible for some of these costs to be apportioned to restricted funds where the terms of the funding specify it or allow it. Fundraising and publicity costs will fall under unrestricted funds for many charities, but it is likely that some of these costs will be charged to restricted funds. For example, a charity running a special appeal can charge the costs of the appeal against that restricted fund.

Grants for the Purchase of Fixed Assets

In the past, the accounting treatment for grants for the purchase of fixed assets in charity accounts has followed Statement of Standard Accounting Practice 4 (SSAP 4). This meant that the grant received (often called a capital grant) was not shown in income when it was received. Instead, it was put into a deferral account on the balance sheet, and an amount was released to income each year to match the depreciation charge on the related asset. The unreleased balance on the deferred income account was either the same value or less than the net book value of the fixed assets, depending on whether the original purchase was fully funded or not. It was really a way of depreciating or amortising the income in the same way as the fixed asset was depreciated. It ensured that the organisation did not have a large surplus in the year the capital grant was received, and then have deficits due to depreciation in each subsequent year.

This treatment does not comply with the SORP. All incoming resources have to be brought into the SOFA when they are received. The recommendation is to put grants for the purchase of fixed assets into the SOFA as a restricted fund. The expenditure on the purchase of the fixed asset will be treated as normal and capitalised on the balance sheet. The depreciation charge each year should be shown as expenditure of the restricted fund. The balance on the restricted fund will represent the "unamortised" amount of the capital grant. The identification of the assets to the fund can be demonstrated on the face of the balance sheet if a columnar format is adopted, or in a note to the accounts.

The advantage of this treatment is that it no longer matters how the fixed assets have been funded; the accounting treatment will be similar. If the purchase of fixed assets has been funded from unrestricted funds, then the identification of assets to funds will show this on the balance sheet or in the note. Charities may choose to designate funds so that the funding of fixed assets is very clear. Readers of accounts may also find the SORP treatment easier to follow, as they will be able to see the full amount of grant income coming into the accounts in the year in which it was received.

Potential problems may arise if readers of accounts assume that the "net incoming resources" are the same as an operating surplus. Net incoming resources will include the incoming resource for the purchase of fixed assets minus the depreciation charge. It is possible therefore to add a section to follow on immediately after the SOFA to show the application of funds on the purchase of fixed assets. The format would show:

◆ the net movement in funds for the year

◆ resources used for net acquisitions of fixed assets for charity use i.e. not investments (distinguishing if necessary between assets for the charity's direct charitable purposes and other purposes)

◆ net movement in funds available for future activities

If preferred this information may be shown in a note to the accounts.

Deferred Income

Charities often receive income before they spend it. It has been common practice for charities to defer income in their accounts so that the income is matched to the expenditure. This is in accordance with fundamental accounting concepts and it is normal accounting practice for commercial enterprises to defer income until the goods have been delivered or the service provided. The income does not go into the income and expenditure account (profit and loss account), but is shown under creditors in the balance sheet as "payments received in advance". This would ensure that commercial enterprises were not taking a profit before it had been earned, following another fundamental accounting concept of "prudence".

In most cases, the SORP will not allow this treatment. Again, the principle to be followed is that all incoming resources should be shown in the SOFA when receivable. Since the SOFA is not trying to show whether there is a surplus or deficit, then the main concern that the enterprise might be taking a profit too early is removed. In fact, the SORP recognises that the risk is that charities will be trying to understate their income, rather than overstate a profit.

If the income is for a particular purpose, then it should be shown as restricted income. The balance of restricted funds at the year end should be explained in a note to the accounts. If the income is part of general income, then the trustees may designate some of the funds and explain the purpose for which the funds will be used. The trustees should also be explaining the charity's financial position in the annual report.

However, there may be circumstances which do require income to be deferred when following the SORP. If the funding is specifically for spending in a subsequent accounting period, then it would be appropriate to defer the income. The income may not be deferred only because the charity does not plan to spend the funds until a later period; it should be a condition of the funding.

Life Subscriptions

Life Subscriptions should be included in income on an appropriate and consistent basis related to the annual subscription. The balance carried forward to subsequent periods should be included in the balance sheet as deferred income under creditors.

Example

A charity has annual subscriptions at £25 per year, or a life subscription for £500. The life subscription equates to 20 years of annual subscriptions. So life subscriptions received should be treated as deferred income, with the amount released each year taken to incoming resources in the SOFA. The deferred income appears on the balance sheet as a creditor.

Gifts in Kind

Gifts in kind are another form of incoming resource and should be included in the SOFA. The exact treatment will depend on the type of gift in kind.

◆ Gifts of assets for distribution by the charity should be recognised as an incoming resource for the year only when distributed, with a corresponding entry to the appropriate expenditure heading. This would apply to charities collecting goods for distribution to the needy, for example in disaster appeals. Where there are undistributed assets at the year end, a description of the items involved and an estimate of their value should be given by way of a note to the accounts.

◆ Gifts of assets for conversion into cash would normally be recognised in the accounting period when receivable. However, this will not always be practicable as the value of the items donated cannot be ascertained until they are sold. This might apply in the case of gifts for raffles and charity auctions as well as charities collecting goods for sale in charity shops. In these case, the income should be included in the accounting period in which the gift is sold.

◆ Gifts of assets for use by the charity (e.g. property for its own occupation) should be recognised as an incoming resource when receivable.

◆ Gifts for retention as investments should also be recognised as an incoming resource when receivable.

A value has to be placed on the gift in kind, but this can be an estimate. For example, if a charity receives a second-hand snooker table as a donation, then it is enough to look through the local papers to get an idea of prices and make your own estimate. Alternatively, shops and dealers may be able to give you a price guide. It is not intended that the charity should incur additional costs by having a professional valuation undertaken, unless the asset is very significant. Properties should normally be valued and it is often helpful to have a condition survey undertaken at the same time. Are you taking on a liability rather than an asset? Gifts in kind of a certain type need to be treated with care and certainly gifts of land and property without the funds to maintain them fall into this category.

If a charity receives donated fixed assets, then the fixed assets should be capitalised and depreciated according to the charity's accounting policies; the value will be included in the accounts as an incoming resource into a restricted fund and the depreciation will be charged against the fund. The accounting treatment will be the same as if the charity had received a specific grant for the purchase of fixed assets.

Intangible Income

This is really similar to gifts in kind and includes volunteers' time or donated facilities. Generally, the SORP does not recommend a change to the current policy for most charities. Volunteers' time does not have to be valued and brought into the accounts as do gifts in kind. It is recommended that the annual report records the amount of intangible income received in this way and takes it into account when summarising the achievements of the year.

Intangible income should not be included in the SOFA unless the charity would otherwise have had to purchase the donated facilities or services. It might be appropriate therefore, to include rent-free premises as a donation in kind. The rental value would be included as a donation under incoming resources and as premises costs under expenditure. The notes to the accounts or the annual report need to explain the accounting policy and further details. Consideration needs to be given to the appropriate policy for donated services such as the printing of annual reports, free legal advice, free technical support. A consistent approach is needed and the narrative part of the annual report needs to pick up on intangible inome not included in the financial statements.

Subsidiary Undertakings

Since many charities undertake fundraising through trading, which is chanelled through subsidiary companies owned by the charity, the SORP recommends that all charities consolidate the subsidiaries into the accounts of the main charity. This sort of trading will typically involve the buying and selling of new goods, or could be the organisation of various fundraising events. The activities themselves are not part of the charity's activities or charitable objects. It is therefore expected that the charity will bring in the profit from those activities into the consolidated SOFA as a separate heading under incoming resources. If the subsidiary remits profits through a deed of covenant or gift aid on a regular basis, then the profits to be brought into the consolidated SOFA and the amount actually remitted may not be very different. The SORP also requires further disclosure in the notes to the accounts, to include the turnover of the subsidiary and the main headings in the profit and loss account.

The recommendation to consolidate applies to all charities and their trading subsidiaries, even if they qualify as "small" under the Companies Acts. So the many charities which have not prepared consolidated accounts in the past on the grounds that the group was small, will now have to do so if they wish to follow the SORP. The argument that the different nature of the activities of the charity and its subsidiary meant that consolidated accounts should not be prepared is not considered valid by the SORP. The "one-line" consolidation method described above is expected to counter this argument.

A charity could also operate through separate entities (usually companies) which are controlled by the charity and are therefore subsidiaries. The subsidiaries can be registered charities themselves, but are not necessarily registered. The activities will fall within the charity's objects and will usually be charitable trading. These subsidiaries should also be consolidated into the accounts of the main charity, but on a "line by line" basis. This means that the gross income is brought in under incoming resources appropriately described, for example, as fees. The costs are then added in to the appropriate headings under expenditure.

It is necessary for every charity to prepare accounts and submit them to the Charity Commission and Companies House if they are registered there. The SORP requires consolidated financial statements ("group accounts") to be prepared. Normal practice is to prepare the balance sheet in a columnar format to show both the consolidated position and the position of the charity itself. If only a consolidated SOFA is presented, sufficient information about the activities of the charity and the profit and loss account of the subsidiary must be given in the notes to the accounts. This is acceptable practice for companies and certainly many of the charities preparing group accounts will also be charitable companies. The example accounts in Chapter 7 illustrate group accounts on this basis. However, the SORP makes it quite clear that consolidated accounts are no substitute for the charity's own accounts.

It will sometimes be difficult to assess whether group accounts are necessary. To be considered a group, one charity should control the activities of the sub-sidiary undertaking. Many charities are connected to other organisations (e.g. a local charity and its national umbrella organisation, or two charities with overlapping boards of trustees). If the relationship falls short of "control", consolidated accounts would not be required, but the nature of the connection, and significant transactions between the connected organisations, should be disclosed. If there are two independent charities, then they would not need to consolidate the accounts, even if the trustees are the same, because charity trustees are required to act independently in the interests of the charity and not to subordinate this to other interests. It is possible that the Charity Commis-sion might direct that the two charities should be treated as one for accounting purposes under section 96(5) or section 96(6) of the Charities Act 1993.

The Charity Commission may also have registered a "subsidiary charity", which is not a subsidiary in the sense used by the Companies Acts. The Commission will normally direct that a subsidiary charity should be accounted for as part of the main charity. It is really a branch and will probably form a restricted fund if the trusts are more narrowly defined than the charity's stated objects.

Branches

The SORP recommends that all branch activities should be reflected in the accounts of the charity. The incoming resources and expenditure of the branch should be brought into the SOFA gross and into the financial year when the transactions arose. It is not acceptable to bring in only the remittances of branches, as and when they are received. The bank account balances of branches also need to be brought into the balance sheet, as do any other assets and liabilities of the charity.

There are three basic types of branches:

◆ an administrative arm of the main charity, which may raise or expend funds on its behalf or in its name. This will be incorporated into the accounts of the main charity as above, with the proviso that funds raised by a branch for a specific purpose or geograpical area will have to be treated as a restricted fund.

◆ funds held under specific trusts by charities will be treated as restricted funds in the accounts of the main charity. The accounts will show movements on these funds just as they would any other restricted fund. Details may be needed in the notes to the accounts.

◆ charitable subsidiaries recognised by the Charity Commission will be branches and incorporated into the accounts of the main charity as above. (These are not the same as subsidiaries under company law, but are parts of the charity which have received separate recognition by the Charity Commission.)

Charities with branches will have to ensure that they obtain sufficient information about the incoming resources and expenditure, gains and losses, assets and liabilities of their branches for the purpose of preparing the annual accounts. It is usual for a form of return to be used so that consistent information is gathered from all the branches.

Definition of Branches in SORP

The SORP provides a framework for identifying branches, setting out the main characteristics of a branch as:

• it uses the name of the main charity within its title
• it exclusively raises funds for the main charity and/or for its own local activities
• it uses the main charity's registration number to receive tax relief on its activities
• it is perceived by the public to be the main charity's local representative
• it receives support from the main charity through advice, publicity, materials etc.

"Branches" which have their own charity registration number are probably not branches, but separate charities. However, there are some cases where subsidiary charities have been given separate registration numbers. It may be necessary to seek clarification form the Charity Commission. Similarly, a charity which is a separate legal entity (such as a company) will not normally be treated as part of the main charity for accounting purposes (except in special circumstances if the Charity Commissioners so direct). It should prepare its own accounts and annual report.

Grants Payable

Charities and foundations which make grants to charities or individuals will show grants payable under direct charitable expenditure. The charity's accounting policy on the recognition of grants payable should be disclosed. Charities may make promises to pay further grants in the future, which are moral, but not legally binding commitments. It is inappropriate under good accounting practice to show these "moral" commitments as accruals. However, the trustees of grant-making charities may wish to earmark part of the unrestricted funds of the charity for these purposes. They would need to create designated funds and explain the purpose in the notes to the accounts.

"Material" grants to institutions must be disclosed. What is material will depend on the size of the grant-making charity and the importance of grant-making to its overall operation. A grant will not be considered material unless it is more than £1,000 and grant-making will be considered material if it makes 5% or more of the total expenditure of the charity. Grant-makers should disclose the 50 largest grants to institutions, providing they are at least £1,000. Grants to individuals do not need to be disclosed.

Where disclosure is necessary, the note to the accounts should show the name of the recipient institution and the total amount of grants paid in the accounting period. Grant-making charities may prefer to disclose all their grants distributed in a separate publication. This is an acceptable alternative to disclosure in the notes to the accounts, providing a note refers to the publication and the total amount paid is reconciled to the accounts figure. There is an "opt out" of public disclosure for the exceptional circumstance where the trustees consider that it would prejudice the furtherance of the charity's objects, or those of recipients. In that case, the charity is required to make the disclosure direct to the Charity Commissioners by providing written particulars of all such grants.

Tax Recoverable

Tax recoverable on covenants and gift aid should be added to the income figure ("grossed up") and shown as a debtor if not yet received by the charity at the end of the financial year.

Revaluation of Investments

The investments have to be grouped by classification for the notes to the accounts, i.e. listed shares, shares in unquoted companies, common investment funds, property, cash.

Investments should be shown at market value in the balance sheet. This means that they have to be revalued at each balance sheet date. The basis of the valuation should be disclosed (e.g. market value). If the investment is property, then the basis of the valuation together with a note to state who undertook the valuation, their qualification and the date of the valuation is required. The notes need to disclose the historical cost of each class of investment.

The gain or loss on revaluing of the investments is taken to the SOFA and shown as an unrealised gain or loss after net incoming resources. An example of this treatment is shown in the example accounts in Chapter 6. The final sale of the investments may give rise to a further gain or loss and this would be reflected in the SOFA under "realised gains and losses".

There are potential conflicts with Financial Reporting Standard 3 (FRS 3) and company legislation, because these both lay down specific requirements in relation to revaluations. Unincorporated charities with no endowment funds can separate the SOFA into two sections, so that the first section deals with revenue income and expenditure, ending with net income/expenditure. The Statement of Total Recognised Gains and Losses should follow straight on, bringing in the net income/expenditure, unrealised gain/loss, funds brought forward and funds carried forward. This layout complies with FRS 3 and is demonstrated in the example in Chapter 6.

Charitable companies have to comply with the Companies Acts requirements for the disclosure of the surplus or deficit excluding unrealised gains or losses. To fulfil this requirement it will therefore be necessary for charitable companies with unrealised gains or losses on the SOFA to produce a summary income and expenditure account in addition to the SOFA. This is illustrated in the examples in Chapter 6 and Chapter 7. The SOFA then fulfils the requirements of FRS 3 to show all recognised gains and losses and a further Statement of Total Recognised Gains and Losses is not required. Companies also have to keep accumulated unrealised gains in a separate reserve, known as the "revaluation reserve". This can be part of the restricted or unrestricted funds, but should be shown separately on the face of the balance sheet and movements explained in the notes to the accounts.

Trustee Remuneration and Expenses

Any amounts paid to trustees must be disclosed in a note to the accounts. The note must be included even if there were no payments, with a statement that the amounts were nil. Remuneration should be disclosed as well as any other benefits whether or not they would be taxable under tax legislation. The reimbursement of expenses should be disclosed by giving the total amount paid in expenses, the type of expenses and the number of trustees receiving the payments.

Staff Emoluments

The SORP calls for disclosure of the average number of staff and their total emoluments. This includes all taxable pay and benefits, using the Inland Revenue definition of emoluments as a guide.

If any staff are receiving more than £40,000 p.a, then this should be disclosed. The requirement is to show the number of staff receiving emoluments in bands of £10,000 commencing with the first band at £40,001 – £50,000. Only bands where there is a disclosure need to be included.

Example

The number of staff receiving emoluments in the following bands were as follows:

£40,001 – £50,000	3
£50,001 – £60,000	2
£70,000 – £80,000	1

This is in contrast to company legislation, which requires the disclosure of total staff costs under the categories of gross pay, social security (employer's national insurance contributions) and other pension contributions. Charitable companies will need to disclose both.

Indemnity Insurance

Where the charity pays the premiums for insurance which indemnifies the trustees or staff against loss arising from negligence, then this fact should be disclosed in a note to the accounts. Note that this is required under the accounting regulations for unincorporated charities whose income exceeds £100,000 per year.

Connected Charities

Any connections with other charities should be explained. A connected charity will be one which has common, parallel or related objects and activities and one of the following conditions exists:

◆ common control (i.e. the same trustees or a majority of trustees who are the same or the same person or persons have the right to appoint a majority of trustees)

◆ unity of administration

Details of connected charities should be given in the annual report, explaining any transactions between them where applicable.

Subsidiaries and associated undertakings should be accounted for by preparing consolidated accounts where the amounts are material. Particulars of the undertaking and their activities must in any case be given in the notes to the accounts.

Transactions with Connected Persons

Any material transactions between the charity and a trustee or a company of which a trustee is a director or shareholder should also be disclosed. Connected persons are defined in the accounting regulations as:

◆ a child, parent, grandchild, grandparent, brother or sister of a trustee

◆ a spouse of a trustee or the spouse of any of the above family members of the trustee

◆ the trustees of non-charitable trusts benefitting a trustee or member of their family

◆ the business partner of a trustee or a member of their family

◆ companies in which a trustee has a substantial interst, i.e. has a significant shareholding and/or is a director

This includes a large number of people and is clearly designed to catch any transactions at all that might not be "at arm's length". If the transaction has been properly undertaken on terms that would be the same for anyone or on terms that are preferential for the charity, then there will not necessarily be a problem. It is required in order that such matters will be out in the open.

Fixed Assets

Fixed assets should be capitalised and depreciated, following normal accounting practice and Statement of Standard Accounting Practice 12 (SSAP 12). It has often been the practice of smaller charities to charge the total cost of the purchase of fixed assets to expenditure. This will only be appropriate if the amount involved is insignificant. Charities should have an accounting policy which determines at what level purchases are considered significant. For example, a charity with gross income of £250,000 should probably have a capitalisation level of about £500. This means that individual items smaller than this will be treated as repairs and renewals and charged to that expenditure headings. Individual items costing more than £250 should be treated as a fixed asset and depreciated over a suitable period, based an the estimated life of the asset. Charities operating in specialist fields should bear in mind their own particular circumstances and come up with a suitable policy. For example, a charity providing temporary accommodation to young people may have to replace bedroom furniture quite quickly, as it is subject to hard wear. It may be better to treat the replacement of bedroom furniture as a regular expenditure item, rather than as a fixed asset. However, the office equipment should be treated as a fixed asset and depreciated.

Some charities are reluctant to charge depreciation on property. The accounting standard states that depreciation should be charged on all "wasting assets" to include buildings. Land does not need to be depreciated, but the buildings do, as they do deteriorate over time. SSAP 12 allows for two situations which would mean that buildings do not have to be depreciated:

◆ where the residual value is greater than the book value (cost or revluation)

◆ where the organisation maintains the building to a sufficient standard such that the market value could be realised

The SORP allows for the special circumstances of certain charities, such as heritage charities. The type of property they own is not a normal type of fixed asset, but may be held under special trusts and frequently the charity may not dispose of the asset. Indeed, the asset often brings with it great liabilities because of the costs of maintenance. It would be misleading to include such assets in the balance sheet as they cannot be realised into cash and they do not represent investments as such. Historic buildings, works of art, special sites may be excluded from the fixed assets for this reason. The accounting policy should explain adequately how such assets are being treated and it may be appropriate to explain more in the annual report.

Assets being purchased under lease purchase, hire purchase or leased under finance leases will be capitalised and depreciated. Gifts in kind which are fixed assets should be brought into fixed assets as if they had been purchased; the corresponding entry in the accounts will be under incoming resources. They should be depreciated as normal.

Summary Income and Expenditure Account

Compliance with Financial Reporting Standard 3 (FRS 3) and company legislation may require a separate statement of income and expenditure in addition to the SOFA. This will be required if:

◆ there are incoming capital resources i.e. new endowment funds in the SOFA for this or the preceding year

◆ there are significant changes in the charity's circumstances, such that there are discontinued operations or acquired operations (in the case of a merger or takeover). These situations are rare in the context of charities and reference should be made to FRS 3 for details of the format of the income and expenditure account required.

◆ there are unrealised gains or losses and the format of the SOFA cannot be adapted to show these after suitable disclosure of the net income/ expenditure

◆ the charity is a company and the disclosure requirements to show net income/expenditure cannot be met within the SOFA

Unincorporated charities with no endowment which does revalue assets can adapt the layout of the SOFA to show the revenue income and expenditure account as the first section of the SOFA, ending with the net income/ expenditure. The Statement of Total Recognised Gains and Losses should then follow, commencing with the net income/expenditure, then showing the unrealised gains/losses, balances on funds brought forward and balances on funds carried forward. This layout is illustrated in Chapter 6.

Charitable companies will not need to prepare a summary income and expenditure account if their SOFA is the same as an income and expenditure account; the additional words "income and expenditure" should be added near the top of the SOFA and the net incoming resources can be described as the net income for the year.

Chapter 4

RECEIPTS AND PAYMENTS BASIS

This chapter includes an example set of accounts in the format recommended by the Charity Commission for a charity choosing to prepare accounts on the receipts and payments basis. There is no prescribed format, as this is not set out in the accounting regulations. In addition, the SORP does not make detailed recommendations. However, the Charity Commission have prepared a guide for charities preparing accounts under the receipts and payments basis: "Accounting for the Smaller Charity". This should be referred to in conjunction with this chapter.

Under section 42 of the Charities Act 1993, the option of preparing simplified accounts on the receipts and payments basis is available to charities meeting the following criteria:

◆ gross income not exceeding £100,000 in the financial year

◆ the charity is not incorporated as a company

The trustees will not be able to exercise the statutory option if the charity's trust deed or constitution prescribes a form of accounts (for example, a constitution may require an income and expenditure account and a balance sheet to be drawn up for each financial year).

The option available to smaller charities enables them to produce a set of accounts in a simplified form instead of producing a statement of financial activities and a balance sheet. This will mean that small charities with relatively straightforward affairs will be able to produce their own financial summary. The Charity Commission also have a standard accounts form for the receipts and payments basis (reproduced on pages 68–73), so charities may complete this instead of preparing their own based on the format given here.

Choosing the Basis of Accounting

Trustees need to consider carefully whether the receipts and payments basis is appropriate for the proper transmission of information to readers of the charity's accounts. The receipts and payments basis is a simplified form of accounting, so it is appropriate for small charities with simple affairs. This is reflected in the example set of accounts in this chapter, which are for a small grant-making foundation. It has no paid staff, no property assets and does not receive grants. It does have a permanent endowment, but the terms of it are very straightforward.

Charities which do have grant income and paid staff, for example, may prefer to prepare annual accounts on the accruals basis. This would then include all costs incurred in the expenditure by category. This may be more appropriate in terms of reporting to grant funders.

The receipts and payments basis does not recognise depreciation, nor can it make allowance for other changes, events and transactions which do not occur through cash, such as revaluations, loan repayments and gifts in kind. The example accounts in Chapter 5 show how financial statements may be drawn up on an accruals basis for a small charity.

Trustees also need to plan ahead if the gross income of the charity is approaching £100,000. It will not be wise to change from the receipts and payments basis to the accruals basis and then back again. Charities close to the threshold would be better to consistently prepare accruals basis accounts. Note also that the requirement to prepare accruals accounts is based on the current year only, unlike the audit requirement, which continues for two further years after the charity has gone below the threshold.

Receipts and payments basis accounts do not attempt to give a "true and fair" view and so an auditor will not be able to give an opinion in those terms. Auditing standards do provide for the case where an audit of accounts on the receipts and payments basis is undertaken, although this will be unusual. Charities which may choose to prepare accounts on the receipts and payments basis will usually choose to have an independent examination, unless the governing instrument specifically requires an audit and has not been amended.

Form and Content of Accounts

Under the receipts and payments basis, the accounts should consist of:

- ◆ an annual report to explain the activities and finances of the charity
- ◆ a receipts and payments account for its general purposes fund and also any endowment or other restricted funds
- ◆ a statement of assets and liabilities, distinguishing between the different funds where applicable
- ◆ notes to the accounts where necessary, e.g. to explain the legal restrictions on any of its funds
- ◆ independent examiner's report or auditor's report

Annual Report

The annual report does have to comply with section 45 of the Charities Act 1993 and regulation 10 of the accounting regulations, although the trustees can take advantage of the reliefs for smaller charities and only have to prepare a brief summary of the activities of the year. They will still have to show all the legal and administrative details, such as the objects of the charity, address, trustees etc. (see Chapter 2 for details of the requirements). The annual report will be very important for many charities preparing accounts on the receipts and payments basis, as additional information may be necessary to ensure a proper understanding of the financial position of the charity.

EXAMPLE REPORT AND ACCOUNTS

The example overleaf shows the way in which the Camberwick Foundation can comply with the accounting regulations and the recommendations in the guide for smaller charities. No example can be used as a template or standard; amendments to the format will always be necessary to reflect the circumstances of the organisation. In particular, the notes may need to be expanded if more explanation is needed or the circumstances require it.

Note that the statement of assets and liabilities is not the same thing as a balance sheet. There is no requirement to value the non-monetary assets, but sufficient narrative information should be given to enable the reader to understand the nature of the assets and their age, state, location and the fund in which they are held. The original cost and the current estimated value can be given if known.

Liabilities may also be noted in narrative form, rather than the form usually adopted in a balance sheet. An estimate of the amount due and when it is due is sufficient.

THE CAMBERWICK FOUNDATION
TRUSTEES' ANNUAL REPORT FOR 1997

The Camberwick Foundation was established by a charitable trust deed on 13 October 1987 and is registered in England and Wales as a charity (number 123456).

The main address for contacts is:

The Old House
Balsam Tree Lane
Livingstone, Worcs.

During 1997, the trustees were:

Archibald Camberwick (Chairman)   Tony Archer (Secretary)
Ann Snell (Treasurer)   Nigel Pargeter

Objects

The charity was established by Lord Camberwick with an endowment of £100,000 with the object of assisting individuals suffering from hardship or distress in the Camberwick area.

Review of Activities

During 1997, the charity has continued to achieve this object by making grants of £59,842 to 242 individuals; a record since the trust was established. Most of the grants help those who are referred by the Social Services Department and the trustees noted a rise in the number of applicants who should be receiving more assistance from the Care in the Community scheme.

The trustees are pleased to report that the trust also achieved another record in 1997; more income was received than in any other year. The trustees are extremely grateful to all the supporters who raise funds and donate to the trust. Without their assistance none of these achievements would have been possible.

Future Plans

The trustees plan to continue the work of the trust in 1998. The investments will be kept under review and some changes made in order to maximise income. The trustees have kept sufficient funds in deposit accounts for approximately one year's distribution of grants. This policy has been reviewed and now the trustees consider that only six months' worth of distributions should be kept in bank accounts that are readily accessible. The rest is to be placed on six month deposit to increase the rate of interest earned. The trustees plan to continue the policy commenced in 1997; that of distributing all income available to the trust in the year.

Trustees' Responsibilities

The trustees recognise their responsibilities for keeping proper accounting records and preparing financial statements each year. The appended accounts have been prepared on the receipts and payments basis and have been examined by an independent examiner, whose report is also appended.

Approved by the Trustees

on.. (date) and signed on their behalf by

.... (Name – Trustee)

INDEPENDENT EXAMINER'S REPORT TO THE TRUSTEES OF THE CAMBERWICK FOUNDATION

I have examined the attached account and statement which have been prepared on the receipts and payments basis.

Respective Responsibilities of Trustees and Examiner

The trustees of the charity are responsible for the preparation of accounts; they consider that the audit requirement under section 43(2) of the Charities Act 1993 does not apply. I have been appointed under section 43 of the Charities Act 1993 and report in accordance with regulations made under section 44 of that Act. It is my responsibility to examine the account and statement, without performing an audit, and to report to the trustees.

Basis of Examiner's Statement

This report is in respect of an examination carried out under section 43 of the Charities Act 1993 and in accordance with the directions given by the Charity Commissioners under section 43(7)(b). An examination includes a review of the accounting records kept by the charity trustees and a comparison of the accounts presented with those records. It also includes a review of the accounts and making such enquiries as are necessary for the purposes of this report. The procedures undertaken do not constitute an audit.

Examiner's Statement

Based on my examination, no matter has come to my attention which gives me reasonable cause to believe that in any material respect accounting records have not been kept in accordance with section 41 of the Charities Act 1993, or that the accounts presented do not accord with those records or comply with the accounting requirements of the Charities Act 1993. No matter has come to my attention in connection with my examination to which, in my opinion, attention should be drawn to enable a proper understanding of the accounts.

A.N. Examiner
Chartered Accountant
Camberwick
Wickshire
30 March 1998

Explanatory Notes
Receipts and Payments Account

Comparative figures should be shown.

The funds should be kept separate i.e. restricted and unrestricted, although there is no prescribed format for doing this. A separate receipts and payments account should be prepared for each fund, i.e. restricted and unrestricted. If there are several restricted funds, these can be grouped together, although there will be a need for the trustees to disclose information about the balance on each restricted fund. This information may be more easily shown in a note to the accounts. The receipts and payments account can be prepared in a columnar form, similar to the format for accruals accounts.

Receipts will be the actual amount of cash received, analysed into suitable categories.

Gifts in kind and intangible income cannot be included, but have to be explained in the trustees' report.

Receipts should be shown gross, rather than net. So fundraising events are the gross receipts before expenses.

Tax recovered by making tax refund claims on covenanted income, gift aid and investment income should be shown as a separate line under receipts. It should be the actual amount received in the year, not the claim arising from that year's income (unless it also happens to have been received).

Receipts may also include items such as loan repayments or the proceeds from the sale of investments or fixed assets. Such receipts should be included in the receipts and payments account under "other receipts", but clearly identified and, if necessary, explained in the notes to the accounts.

Payments should be grouped into headings which help to make sense of the charity's activities, rather than lists of the headings in the cash book, such as rent, rates, light and heat. The headings suggested are:

- grants made to beneficiaries (individuals and institutions)
- loans to beneficiaries
- publicity and education about the charity's cause
- services provided to beneficiaries
- fundraising and publicity
- management and administration
- purchase of fixed assets for the charity's use
- purchase of investments
- other, e.g. loan repayments, hire purchase payments

The net receipts or net payments can be reconciled to the bank balances for the fund, but it is not a requirement.

THE CAMBERWICK FOUNDATION
RECEIPTS AND PAYMENTS ACCOUNT – GENERAL FUND
For the year ended 31 December 1997

	1997 £	1996 £
Receipts		
Donations	41,950	40,134
Fundraising Events	13,711	16,346
Investment Income	5,946	6,997
Income Tax Recovered	3,489	–
	65,096	63,477
Payments		
Direct charitable:		
Grants to Beneficiaries	59,842	41,294
Other expenditure:		
Fundraising and Publicity Costs	1,873	1,623
Management and Administration	2,294	2,059
Purchase of Equipment	–	4,000
	64,009	48,976
Excess of Receipts over Payments	1,087	14,501
Cash and Bank Deposits Brought Forward	63,165	48,664
Cash and Bank Deposits Carried Forward	64,252	63,165

Approved by the trustees on

.... (date) and signed on their behalf by

.... (Name of Trustee)

Explanatory Notes
The Statement of Assets and Liabilities

Cash and Bank Deposits should be shown as the first item in the list of assets and liabilities. The separate accounts do not have to be shown, but the accounts belonging to the different funds of the charity do need to be identified.

Other Monetary Assets will include any amounts of money owed to the charity. This may include sums due from the Inland Revenue for a tax claim submitted, but not yet paid. This will not have been counted in the receipts. The fund to which the assets belong should be identified.

Investment Assets will include cash on fixed term deposit, shares, property held to generate rental income or for capital growth. Sufficient information should be given to enable a reader to understand the nature of the assets and in which fund they are held. A proper description of the assets should be given. The market value can be given, but is not required.

Fixed Assets Used by the Charity should be shown separately from investment assets. Particulars of the items held, their location and condition should be given. It is not necessary to value the items, but the estimated value can be given if known.

Liabilities will include unpaid bills of the organisation, loans from others, amounts due under hire purchase agreements. They should only include amounts due at the date of the accounts. These should be separated if possible into amounts due within twelve months of the year end (Current Liabilities) and longer te.m liabilities (Future Liabilities)

Commitments may be shown in the Statement of Assets and Liabilities. These may include promises to pay grants, plans for building works or obligations under operating leases, but only if they represent binding obligations to pay.

Contingent Liabilities should be explained in the Statement of Assets and Liabilities. The nature of the contingency, the likely outcome, and the amount involved should be given. Contingencies might include guarantees given on behalf of other charities, outstanding lawsuits or industrial tribunal cases.

THE CAMBERWICK FOUNDATION
STATEMENT OF ASSETS AND LIABILITIES
As at 31 December 1997

	1997 £	1996 £
Cash and Bank Deposits - General Fund		
Bank – Capital Reserve Deposit Account	42,256	54,311
Bank – Business Reserve Deposit Account	2,580	2,532
Bank – Current Accounts	14,961	5,165
Cash in Hand	4,455	1,157
	64,252	63,165
Other Monetary Assets - General Fund		
Loans to Beneficiaries	2,000	2,000
Tax Claim Outstanding	6,498	3,489
	8,498	5,489

Investment Assets

Investment assets are government stocks and shares of UK companies having paid a dividend in each of the last five years. The market value of the investments was £159,324 at 31 December 1997. The investments represent the £100,000 endowment of Lord Camberwick, whose settlement established the foundation. The permanent endowment of £100,000 is to be invested to produce an income which may be used for the beneficiaries of the charity.

Fixed Assets used by the Charity

In 1996, computer equipment was purchased for £4,000 to assist in the administration of the charity.

Current Liabilities

1997 expenses due were £929

Approved by the trustees on

.... (date) and signed on their behalf by

.... (Name of Trustee)

Explanatory Notes
Notes to the Accounts

The accounting basis should be clearly explained, i.e.that the receipts and payments basis has been used.

Most accounting standards do not apply to receipts and payments accounts and so no reference should be made to them. In addition, the SORP mostly applies to accruals accounts and so no reference is made to it.

The types of funds held by the charity should be explained, i.e according to whether the charity has endowment, restricted and unrestricted funds. The note should explain the terms of the trusts on which the funds are held and any assets which represent the fund balances.

Explanations on the basis of the categories of the payments should be given to assist the reader of the accounts.

Grants paid should be listed if these are to institutions, but is not necessary if the grants are to individuals. The SORP recommends that the largest 50 grants are detailed showing the name of the institution receiving the grant. This requirement is waived when the amounts are less than £1,000 or grant-giving is an insignificant part of an organisation's activity.

Cash and Bank Deposits – the note explains which fund the assets belong to if this is not stated on the Statement of Assets and Liabilities itself.

Other Monetary Assets – additional information which may further a proper understanding should be given.

THE CAMBERWICK FOUNDATION
NOTES TO THE ACCOUNTS
For the year ended 31 December 1997

1. **Accounting Basis**

   These accounts have been prepared on the receipts and payments basis.

2. **Unrestricted Funds**

   All receipts and payments relate to general unrestricted funds. The investment income arises from the investments which are held in the permanent endowment fund. The terms of the endowment allow income to be used for grants to beneficiaries of the charity.

3. **Management and Administration Costs**

   Management and administration costs relate to postage, printing, stationery and the general costs of administering the trust. The trustees give all their time free of charge.

4. **Fundraising and Publicity Costs**

   Fundraising and publicity costs are the direct costs of fundraising events.

5. **Cash and Bank Deposits**

   All cash and bank deposits are held in the unrestricted general funds.

6. **Monetary Assets**

   Loans to beneficiaries are interest free and with no fixed repayment date; all relate to the unrestricted general funds of the charity.

Receipts & Payments Account and
Statement of Assets & Liabilities
under Section 42(3) of the Charities Act 1993

ACC-1371

Charity
Commissioners
for England and Wales

Charity Reference

Charity Name
(please print)

**Charity Commission
Number** (if registered)

**For the financial
year to**   /   /

Declaration

The account set out on page(s) 2,3 and 4* / 5* for the financial year (being the
period of . . . months)* ended on the above date, and the statement of assets
and liabilities at that date set out on page 6 (together with continuation sheets
numbered . . . to . . . attached)* are approved by the trustees.
*Delete as appropriate

Signature

Date   /   /

Trustee authorised to sign on behalf of all trustees

Full Name
(BLOCK CAPITALS)

Forwarded by

Address

**Daytime Telephone
Number**
(in case of any query)

This Account and Statement, together with any auditor's or independent
examiner's report, be attached to the trustees' annual report for the year
to be filed with the Charity Commissioners for England & Wales not later than ten
months from the end of the financial year (as above) in the case of a registered
charity with gross income or expenditure for the year exceeding £10,000.

Notes for completing this form

This form should only be used for a charity which is not a limited company and
whose gross recorded income for the financial year from all sources, including
special trusts, does not exceed £100,000. Where there are no restricted funds of
any kind administered as part of the charity, only sections A and D (pages 2, 3
and 6) should be completed.

Please read the notes on the insert sheet before beginning to fill in this form.

Continuation sheets, if used, should be numbered sequentially and a reference
note made on the page to which they relate (eg, "see continuation sheet 1,
reference section A2b" or "see continuation sheet 2, reference section B").

1

Section A	General Fund(s) unrestricted by donors

Charity Commission Number

Charity Name (please print)

Financial year ending
/ /

Please read the notes on the accompanying sheet **before** completing this page.

A1 Receipts

This year's amount*

Last Year's amount*

(*Round to nearest whole £)
£   £

A1a Voluntary Sources

+   +

A1b Trading Activities

+   +

A1c Income from Assets

Sub total
A1 (a+b+c)

+   +

A1d Miscellaneous Receipts

Total Receipts for Section A1

Please use a continuation sheet where space is lacking

2

Section A   General Fund(s) unrestricted by donors - continued

Charity Commission Number	Charity Name (please print)	Financial year ending
		/ /

Please read the notes on the accompanying sheet **before** completing this page.

A2 Payments

	This year's amount*	Last Year's amount*
	(*Round to nearest whole £)	
	£	£

A2a Direct Charitable Expenditure

+

A2b Other Expenditure

Sub total
A2 (a+b)

+   +

A2c Payments for Investment and Other Assets

+   +

A2d Miscellaneous Payments

Total Payments for Section A2

A3 Balance(s) brought forward from last year

Balance(s) in hand (Section D1a)
(Total for A1-Total for A2+Amount at A3)

Please use a continuation sheet where space is lacking

Section B   Restricted Fund(s) - to be completed only if applicable

Charity Commission Number	Charity Name (please print)	Financial year ending
		/ /

Please read the notes on the accompanying sheet **before** completing this page.

B1 Receipts

This year's amount*   Last Year's amount*
(*Round to nearest whole £)
£   £

B1a Voluntary Sources (specify restriction)

+   +

B1b Income from Restricted Fund Assets

Sub total (a+b)

+   +

B1c Miscellaneous Receipts

Total Receipts Section B1

B2 Payments

B2a Direct Charitable Expenditure

+   +

B2b Other Expenditure

+   +

B2c Payments for Investment and Other Assets

+   +

B2d Miscellaneous Payments

Total Payments for Section B2

+   +

B3 Balance(s) brought forward from last year

Balance(s) in hand (Section D1a)
(Total for B1-Total for B2+Amount at B3)

Please use a continuation sheet where space is lacking

4

Section C	Permanent Endowment(s) - to be completed only if applicable

Charity Commission Number	Charity Name (please print)	Financial year ending
		/ /

Please read the notes on the accompanying sheet **before** completing this page.

C1 Capital Receipts

This year's amount* Last Year's amount*
(*Round to nearest whole £)

C1a Voluntary Sources (state terms of trust)

+

+

C1b Miscellaneous Receipts

Total Capital Receipts for Section C1

C2 Payments

C2a Amount converted to Income (give Authority)

+

+

C2b Payments for Investment and Other Assets

+

+

C2c Miscellaneous Payments

Total Capital Payments for Section C2

+

+

C3 Balance(s) brought forward from last year

Balance(s) in hand (Section D1a)
(Total for C1-Total for C2+Amount at C3)

Please use a continuation sheet where space is lacking

Section D	Statement of Assets & Liabilities as at the Financial Year-End

Charity Commission Number	Charity Name (please print)	Financial year ending
		/ /

Please read the notes on the accompanying sheet **before** completing this page.

D1   Monetary Assets

	General £	Restricted £	Endowments £

D1a   Cash Balances on Receipts & Payments Account(s) carried forward

(Round to nearest whole £)

Total Cash Balances

Total of Cash Balances must agree with Sections A, B & C

D1b   Other Monetary Assets

D2   Liabilities

D2a   Liabilities now due for payment

	Fund (code)	Date of origin	When payable	Estimated amount £

D2b   Future & Contingent Liabilities

		/ /	/ /	
		/ /	/ /	
		/ /	/ /	

D3   Non Monetary Assets

	Fund (code)	Date acquired	Cost to Date (if known)	Current value (if known)

D3a   Held for Investment Purposes

		/ /		
		/ /		
		/ /		
		/ /		

D3b   Held for the Charity's own use

		/ /		
		/ /		
		/ /		
		/ /		

Please use a continuation sheet where space is lacking

6

V1 10/95

Chapter 5

SMALL CHARITY ACCOUNTS – ACCRUALS BASIS

Unincorporated charities with gross income up to £100,000 may choose to prepare accounts on the receipts and payments basis rather than the accruals basis. However, this option is not open to all charities. The trust deed or constitution of some unincorporated charities may require an income and expenditure account and a balance sheet to be prepared annually, which implies accruals basis accounts. All charitable companies have to prepare accounts on the accruals basis.

The Statement of Recommended Practice (SORP) does not make allowances for smaller charities preparing accruals accounts and so the SORP has to be followed in full. However, the Charity Commission have produced a guide "Accruals Accounting for th Smaller Charity" aimed at charities with income up to £100,000. It is a digest of the full SORP and the accounting regulations, omitting the matters which are likely to be relevant only to larger charities. It is a helpful and easy to read guide and contains two example sets of accounts.

Choosing the Basis of Accounting

It is also a matter to be carefully considered by trustees. If the charity is close to the £100,000 threshold, it may be simpler to adopt the accruals basis so that there are no complications at the year end. It will also not be easy to change from receipts and payments basis to accruals basis, and then back again. The two methods of accounting are incompatible and comparative figures will have to be restated on the new accounting basis.

It may also be wise to adopt the accruals basis if the charity receives grant funding or employs staff. Grant funders need to be shown accounts where they can readily see that the grant has been properly used for the purposes for which it was given; if some liabilities were outstanding at the year end this may not be apparent from a receipts and payments account.

Form and Content of Accounts

Under the accruals basis, the report and accounts should consist of:

◆ an annual report to explain the activities and finances of the charity

◆ a statement of financial activities showing the incoming resources and application of resources on all funds

◆ a summary income and expenditure (only in certain cases)

◆ a balance sheet

- notes to the accounts as required
- audit report or independent examiner's statement

Annual Report

The annual report does have to comply with section 45 of the Charities Act 1993 and regulation 10 of the accounting regulations, although the trustees can take advantage of the reliefs for smaller charities and only have to prepare a brief summary of the activities of the year. They will still have to show all the legal and administrative details, such as the objects of the charity, address, trustees etc. (see Chapter 2 for details of the requirements). The example annual report which follows assumes that an audit is carried out, and therefore includes a full statement of the trustees' responsibilities in relation to the accounts and financial matters.

Example Report and Accounts

This chapter looks at a simple set of accounts prepared under the accruals basis. The charity is unincorporated and has gross income of less than £100,000. Most income is unrestricted, since it receives grants and donations for its main charitable purpose, that of running a community centre. The restricted funds received in the year are a grant and donation specifically for equipment. The donation is kitchen equipment given to the community centre, so it is a gift in kind. The example shows that this is valued (best estimate is sufficient) and included in the Statement of Financial Activities (SOFA) under incoming resources. It is also shown as an addition to fixed assets and depreciated. This is to treat the donation in kind in the same way as if the donor had given cash and the centre had then purchased the kitchen equipment.

Otherwise, the SOFA is very similar to an old-style income and expenditure account. The expenditure may be shown under old-style headings as in the example, but charities may use the new headings of direct charitable expenditure, fundraising and publicity, management and administration. (See Chapter 3 and Glossary for definitions of those terms; see Chapter 6 for an example set of accounts demonstrating the layout.)

No summary income and expenditure account is required, as the only items included in the SOFA relate to income and expenditure. A summary income and expenditure account would be required if there were endowment transactions, which would be excluded from the summary income and expenditure to arrive at the net income for the year. If the charity were incorporated, then a summary income and expenditure account would also be required if there were any revaluations of assets.

CAMBERWICK COMMUNITY CENTRE
TRUSTEES' ANNUAL REPORT
For the year ended 31 March 1997

Legal and Administrative Details

Status: Unincorporated association established on 1 September 1983 and registered as a charity on 4 January 1984.

Principal Address: St. Stephen's
Camberwick Green
Greater Camberwick
Wickshire

Trustees: Elvis Cridlington (Chairman)
Penny Morris (Vice-Chairman)
Trevor Evans (Secretary)
Marcus Steele (Treasurer)
Holly Oakes
Mavis Wright
Jim Broadside
Angus Wiltshire
Adrian Homer
Bill Coventry
Kim Sullivan
Sue Hammond

Objects of the charity: To relieve poverty by providing educational, recreational and social activities to the inhabitants of the area of Camberwick.

Activities and Review of the Year

The past year has seen considerable development of activities through the efforts of Jane Ayrshire, our development worker. She commenced in post in August 1995 with funding from the Borough of Camberwick. Her post has been established to expand the range of activities and different groups active in the borough. The real success of her work is told through the statistics: we now have 20 different groups involving hundreds of people of different ages in all sorts of activities.

We are grateful to the parish of St. Stephen's for allowing us to use the church hall for the majority of our activities. We hope that the development of a new community centre close by will enable us to return so many favours. In particular we would like to thank Rev. James and his wife for all their time and efforts.

We must also thank the many volunteers who give their time to the various projects and outings. In total this represents hours of work which cannot possibly be valued, but without which the centre would not exist.

One of the significant developments of 1996/97 was the receipt of funding to buy chairs and tables for use in the church hall and later in the new centre. The Watkins Group kindly donated kitchen equipment no longer in use at their staff

➤ *CONTINUED*

➤ *CONTINUED*

canteen, which we estimate would have cost £3,800 to buy secondhand. The acquisition of the catering capacity cooker will enable a great expansion of food preparation on the premises, once the health and safety improvements to the facilities have been made.

The Community Centre continues to move forward with its plans to establish a centre in its own premises by the year 2000. The feasibility study for the centre has been completed by the Camberwick College of Further Education and makes positive recommendations in favour of the site to the south of the Green. The trustees will be developing more detailed plans to take this project forward and raise the necessary funding.

Trustees' Responsibilities

Under the Charities Act 1993, the trustees are required to prepare a statement of accounts for each financial year which gives a true and fair view of the state of affairs of the charity at the end of the financial year and of the incoming resources and application of resources in the year. In preparing the statement, the trustees are required to:

- select suitable accounting policies and apply them consistently;
- make judgements and estimates that are reasonable and prudent;
- state whether applicable accounting standards and statements of recommended practice have been followed, subject to any material departures disclosed and explained in the statement of accounts.
- prepare the financial statements on the going concern basis unless it is inappropriate to presume that the charity will continue its operations

The trustees are responsible for keeping proper accounting records which disclose with reasonable accuracy at any time the financial position of the charity at that time and to enable the trustees to ensure that any statement of account prepared by them complies with the regulations under section 42(1) of the Charities Act 1993. They are also responsible for safeguarding the assets of the trust and hence for taking reasonable steps for the prevention and detection of fraud and other irregularities.

Approved by the Trustees on

.... (date) and signed on their behalf by

.... (Name – Trustee)

Explanatory Notes
Statement of Financial Activities

This charity has no capital incoming resources, so the sub-heading "income and expenditure" can also be used to explain that only revenue items are included in the SOFA. Note that grants or donations for the purchase of fixed assets are not capital resources.

Most of the **incoming resources** are unrestricted, as is the expenditure.

The **grant income** which is restricted is for the purchase of equipment.

The **donations** which are restricted all relate to a donation in kind, which is explained further in note 7.

The **expenditure** is shown in the "natural" classification, which is probably no change to the charity's previous practice.

The **expenditure on the restricted fund** is the depreciation of the equipment purchased with the restricted income funds.

The **net income** for the year on unrestricted funds is the same as a surplus on income and expenditure in this example.

The **SOFA** must show the fund balances (reserves) brought forward and carried forward.

The **statement at the foot of the SOFA** is a requirement of Financial Reporting Standard 3 (FRS 3).

Comparative figures for the preceding year should be shown, although these do not have to be split into restricted and unrestricted funds.

CAMBERWICK COMMUNITY CENTRE
STATEMENT OF FINANCIAL ACTIVITIES
For the year ended 31 March 1997

	Notes	Unrestricted £	Restricted £	Total £	1996 £
Income and Expenditure					
Incoming Resources					
Grants	2	24,800	2,200	27,000	14,000
Donations		2,900	3,800	6,700	3,050
Bank Interest		235	–	235	105
		27,935	6,000	33,935	17,155
Resources Expended					
Staff Costs	3	16,530	–	16,530	10,459
Projects		1,567	–	1,567	1,058
Outings		1,492	–	1,492	1,235
Telephone and Postage		843	–	843	643
Printing and Stationery		1,529	–	1,529	592
Insurance		858	–	858	783
Travel		305	–	305	262
Volunteers' Expenses		648	–	648	528
Accountancy		700	–	700	500
Examiner's Fees		250	–	250	–
Depreciation		–	1,200	1,200	–
		24,722	1,200	25,922	16,060
Net Income for the Year		3,213	4,800	8,013	1,095
Funds at 1 April 1996		10,018	–	10,018	8,923
Funds at 31 March 1997		13,231	4,800	18,031	10,018

All the charity's operations are classed as continuing. Movements on reserves and all recognised gains and losses are shown above.

Explanatory Notes
Balance Sheet

This example shows the balance sheet in columnar form, to show which assets belong to each fund. This format is optional, but the information must be given in a note if not given in this form.

Fixed Assets are shown in the restricted fund. These are the assets purchased with the restricted grant and the donated assets.

Debtors are the amounts due to the charity at the balance sheet date and should all be recoverable. Provision should be made for any bad debts.

Cash at Bank includes all bank accounts, deposit and current, as well as the balance in the petty cash at the balance sheet date.

Creditors: Amounts Falling Due Within One Year are the current liabilities of the charity.

Net Current Assets are calculated as the difference between the total current assets and the creditors falling due within one year.

Net Assets totals the fixed assets and the net current assets. This figure should always be the same as the total funds of the charity.

Funds is the part of the balance sheet which summarises all the balances of the funds. The figures here should agree to the bottom line on the SOFA.

Approved by… The accounts must be approved at a meeting of the trustees. At least one trustee signs the balance sheet on behalf of all trustees.

CAMBERWICK COMMUNITY CENTRE
BALANCE SHEET
As at 31 March 1997

	Notes	Unrestricted £	Restricted £	Total £	1996 £
Fixed Assets	4	–	4,800	4,800	–
Current Assets					
Debtors	5	1,432	–	1,432	982
Cash at Bank		14,347	–	14,347	12,452
		15,779	–	15,779	13,434
Creditors: **Amounts Falling Due Within One Year**	6	(2,548)	–	(2,548)	(3,416)
Net Current Assets		13,231	–	13,231	10,018
Net Assets		13,231	4,800	18,031	10,018
Funds					
Unrestricted Funds		13,231	–	13,231	10,018
Restricted Funds	7	–	4,800	4,800	–
Total Funds		13,231	4,800	18,031	10,018

Approved by the trustees on

.... (date) and signed on their behalf by

.... (Name of Trustee)

Explanatory Notes
Notes to the Accounts

Accounting policies must be described for all relevant matters.

a) It is taken for granted that the accounts are prepared on the accruals basis and follow other fundamental accounting concepts. The reference to applicable accounting standards confirms this, however, but also confirms compliance with many other standards. The auditor or independent examiner has to check that the accounts do comply with these standards.

There should also be a statement that the SORP is being followed. For clarification, the date of the final version of the SORP has been included.

b) Voluntary income – confirmation that all donations and gifts are included in the SOFA when received. Explanation that gifts in kind are also included at valuation.

c) Intangible income needs a policy, depending on the type of organisation. Many charities receive voluntary assistance and this cannot usually be valued or included in the accounts. Further details should be given in the trustees' report.

d) Grants – need to explain the basis for inclusion. A statement similar to the one for voluntary income may be sufficient, but consider whether there are any particular circumstances or policies. The example explains the treatment of grants for the purchase of fixed assets.

e) Restricted funds will need an accounting policy to explain how the charity identifies such funds.

f) Unrestricted funds need to be explained as appropriate, clarifying any terminology used by the charity.

g) Depreciation – the policy has to be set out and the rate of depreciation stated i.e the number of years of useful life assets are assumed to have or the percentage used.

Note 2 – Grants

This note gives further information on the source of grants and their purpose. Where the list is lengthy, then it should be made clear which grants are restricted income and which are unrestricted. Further information may be added if required by the funders, such as an explanation of the application of funds.

Note 3 – Staff Emoluments

The total amount paid to staff by way of pay and benefits in kind must be disclosed in the note to the accounts. In this example, there are no benefits so the gross pay is the same as the emoluments. For the sake of clarity, the national insurance contributions are shown, so that the figure in the accounts can be readily reconciled to the figure in the note. The average number of staff employed in the year should also be given. You can add more information about the posts the staff held, whether they are full-time or part-time, or other information you think will assist a reader of the accounts.

CAMBERWICK COMMUNITY CENTRE
NOTES TO THE ACCOUNTS
FOR THE YEAR ENDED 31 MARCH 1997

1. Accounting Policies

a) The accounts have been prepared in accordance with applicable accounting standards and follow the recommendations in Statement of Recommended Practice: Accounting by Charities (SORP) issued October 1995.

b) Voluntary income is received by way of donations and gifts and is included in full in the Statement of Financial Activities when received. Gifts in kind are valued at their estimated value to the charity and included under the appropriate headings.

c) Intangible income is valued and included in income to the extent that it represents goods or services which would otherwise be purchased. Where it is not possible to value the goods or services, such as volunteer time, the accounts do not include them.

d) Grants including grants for the purchase of fixed assets are recognised in full in the Statement of Financial Activities in the year in which they are received.

e) Restricted funds are to be used for specified purposes as laid down by the donor. Expenditure which meets these criteria is identified to the fund.

f) Unrestricted funds are donations and other income received or generated for the objects of the charity without further specified purpose and are available as general funds.

g) Fixed assets are for use by the charity in fulfilling its main charitable objects and are capitalised and depreciated. Depreciation is provided on all fixed assets at rates calculated to write of the cost of each asset over its estimated useful life, which in all cases is set at five years.

2. Grants

	1997 £	1996 £
Borough of Camberwick:		
For Camberwick Community Centre	24,800	14,000
For the purchase of equipment	2,200	–
	27,000	14,000

3. Staff Emoluments

	1997	1996
Total Emoluments – Gross Salary of development worker	15,000	9,491
National Insurance Contributions	1,530	968
Total cost to charity	16,530	10,459

One development worker was employed throughout 1996/97 and for part of 1995/96.

Note 4 – Fixed Assets

The fixed assets are shown in two categories, as the source of funding was separate. This is not absolutely necessary, as the rate of depreciation is the same for both categories and they are both equipment. It is necessary to show separately assets which are very different in nature, so freehold land and buildings, leasehold land and buildings, equipment and motor vehicles would be in separate categories. Cost, depreciation and net book value should be shown as brought forward figures, change in year and carried forward figure.

Note 5 – Debtors

Any breakdown of the debtors total shown on the balance sheet which will help a reader to understand the nature of the amounts due should be given. The minimum required is an analysis into:

- trade debtors
- amounts owed by connected bodies
- other debtors
- prepayments

Note 6 – Creditors

It is a requirement to show separately in this note:

- loans and overdrafts
- trade creditors
- amounts due to any connected body
- other creditors
- accruals and deferred income

Headings may be omitted where there is nothing to state against them.

Note 7 – Restricted Funds

The note needs to explain what the total balance carried forward in the balance sheet relates to. It is helpful to identify the source of the restricted fund and how it will be used in the future. In this case the funds have been applied to the purchase of the fixed assets and so do not represent unspent cash funds. The grant conditions applying in this case have been further explained.

Note 8 – Trustees' Remuneration and Expenses

A note must be included even if the amounts of both remuneration and expenses were nil. There is no need to detail who received the expenses, but the total paid out and the nature of the expenses should be stated. Trustees should not be remunerated unless special consent has been given by the Charity Commission and it is permitted under the governing instrument.

CAMBERWICK COMMUNITY CENTRE
NOTES TO THE ACCOUNTS
FOR THE YEAR ENDED 31 MARCH 1997

4. Fixed Assets

	Centre Furniture £	Kitchen Equipment £	Total £
COST			
Additions in year and at 31 March 1997	2,200	3,800	6,000
DEPRECIATION			
Provided in year and at 31 March 1997	440	760	1,200
NET BOOK VALUE			
At 31 March 1997	1,760	3,040	4,800

5. Debtors

	1997 £	1996 £
Tax recoverable on covenanted donations	332	282
Prepayments	1,100	700
	1,432	982

6. Creditors: Amounts Falling Due Within One Year

	£	£
Creditors	968	432
Accruals	1,580	2,984
	2,548	3,416

7. Restricted Funds

The balances on restricted funds consisted of the following funds carried forward to fund future depreciation:

	Incoming	Outgoing	At 31 March 1997
a) Donated kitchen equipment	3,800	760	3,040
b) Furniture for the community centre funded by a specific grant	2,200	440	1,760
	6,000	1,200	4,800

The conditions of the grant stipulate that the assets purchased must be returned to the grant funder if the charity ceases to function within five years of the grant payment, or the funds must be returned in full if the charity sells the equipment.

8. Trustees' Remuneration and Expenses

None of the trustees were remunerated. Five trustees received £423 (1996 – £505) as reimbursement for costs such as stationery, telephone and postage.

Chapter 6

MEDIUM SIZED CHARITY

In this chapter are some accounts drawn up in the format required by the SORP. They are an example and you will need to think about your own circumstances and amend the format accordingly. The notes to the accounts are a part of them and you do need to consider carefully all that is required in the notes; they add significantly to the overall information value of the accounts. Add notes if you think they will help the reader to understand your financial position; you do not have to only do the minimum necessary. The particular circumstances of the charity may require further notes and disclosure and the checklist in Appendix I should assist you to identify any further requirements.

Content of Accounts

A set of accounts or financial statements should consist of the following:

◆ Annual Report of the Trustees (Directors' Report)

◆ Statement of Financial Activities

◆ Summary Income and Expenditure Account (for some charities)

◆ Balance Sheet

◆ Cashflow Statement (only a requirement for large organisations)

◆ Notes to the Accounts

◆ Auditor's Report

The annual report for the example organisation in this chapter is in Chapter 2, but it should be remembered that it is part of the financial statements as a whole. The auditor's report is not included in this example, but example reports are given in Chapter 8.

An example of a cashflow statement is included in Chapter 7.

Example Accounts

The example accounts in this chapter illustrate a charity operating in a fairly simple way: – gross income of just over £270,000

◆ grant and contract income

◆ restricted, unrestricted and designated funds

◆ no endowment (capital) funds

◆ small amount of investments

◆ no trading subsidiary

◆ no significant fundraising activity

◆ shop selling donated goods

These accounts are in their final form and before you get to this stage you will have to prepare some detailed working papers. There are also implications for the bookkeeping records, as the format of these may need to be amended so that they produce the information required. In particular, you will need to think about the categories of expenditure; the usual headings will still apply, but in addition, cost centre analysis is required. That is, the expenditure has to be grouped into the activities of the organisation. Many charities already undertake this type of analysis so that they can cost out activities more effectively and report to funders. It is best to keep to a format that is useful for management accounting and adapt this to meet the requirements of the SORP.

In this example, we were able to identify two areas of direct charitable activity as belonging to restricted funds and one area of direct charitable activity as belonging to unrestricted funds. In addition, we identified the fundraising and publicity costs and most of the management and administration costs as belonging to unrestricted funds. It may not always be quite as simple as this, and certain projects may receive a mix of funding, both unrestricted and restricted. It is possible to choose to put the whole activity into restricted funds and then "top-up" the funding of it by transferring some unrestricted income to restricted funds. Any such transfer would be shown below Net Incoming Resources for the Year. The example in Chapter 7 shows this treatment.

The charity has a shop selling donated goods and separate lines for this income and expenditure have been shown, in order that the net result on the shop activity can easily be ascertained. This is not a requirement, and the alternative would be to show this information in a note to the accounts. In this example, there are no sales of "bought-in" goods. If the level of sales of bought-in goods exceeded 10% of the total income, then this would be a potentially taxable activity. It would also mean that the activity would probably be significant enough to require separate disclosure as non-charitable trading.

This example includes a summary income and expenditure account, as this is a charitable company and Companies Acts requirements are thereby fulfilled. An alternative SOFA is given at the end of the example accounts, to show the layout which could be adopted for an unincorporated charity, removing the need for a separate summary income and expenditure account. This layout allows an unincorporated charity to comply with Financial Reporting Standard 3 (FRS 3).

Explanatory Notes
Statement of Financial Activities (SOFA)

A columnar format has been adopted to show movements on restricted and unrestricted funds. An additional column would be needed if the charity had capital (endowment) funds. Designated funds do not require a separate column because they are part of the unrestricted funds, but you may choose to show these as a separate column.

Comparative figures should be shown for the preceding year; these do not have to be analysed into restricted and unrestricted funds. However, note that you will have to calculate the balance brought forward on each fund. Therefore, you may need to re-work the preceding year's figures to obtain the balance sheet position. You will also have to re-work the income and expenditure account for the preceding year into the new categories of expenditure.

Local authority contracts are fees from charitable trading. Whilst the fees are for services specified in the contracts, they are not donated funds held on special trust, and so will be unrestricted rather than restricted.

Charity shop – donated goods income is shown on a separate line. The requirement is to show this form of income as part of voluntary income, but the information value of the SOFA may be enhanced if extra lines are inserted. This would not be appropriate if the amounts were immaterial.

Investment income is split between restricted and unrestricted income. The income from the investments belongs to the unrestricted funds. The bank deposit interest earned during the year is split between the two funds on an estimated basis, according to the average amount held on deposit from each fund during the year. They do not have a separate deposit account for restricted funds.

Direct Charitable Expenditure is further broken down into the three main areas of activity for this charity.

Fundraising and Publicity – If there is no expenditure on fundraising and publicity, then this heading may be omitted. Fundraising costs could be allocated to both restricted and unrestricted funds, depending on the nature of the restricted funds and the type of fundraising. For example, the restriction may exist because the funds may only be used in a particular geographical area, but they were raised from an appeal, the costs of which can be identified.

Shop operating costs are separated out from the other fundraising costs, as this is more informative.

Management and Administration will be a heading for nearly every charity and will usually be part of the unrestricted funds, although they could be apportioned to restricted funds if this was within the terms of the funding.

Total Resources Expended – A note to the accounts should give the analysis of expenditure into the natural headings, and the note number by Total Resources Expended refers the reader to this note.

ELDERLY CONCERN CAMBERWICK
STATEMENT OF FINANCIAL ACTIVITIES
For the year ended 31 March 1997

	Notes	Restricted £	Unrestricted £	Total £	1996 £
Incoming Resources					
Grants	2	150,000	–	150,000	126,132
Local Authority Contracts		-	95,000	95,000	80,414
Donations	3	-	5,000	5,000	6,796
Charity shop – donated goods		20,000	-	20,000	18,000
Investment Income		765	900	1,665	1,324
Total Incoming Resources		155,765	115,900	271,665	232,666
Resources Expended					
Direct Charitable Expenditure					
Advice and Advocacy		68,917	-	68,917	61,756
Domiciliary Care		68,391	-	68,391	53,316
Luncheon Club		90,795	-	90,795	63,433
		137,308	90,795	228,103	178,505
Other Expenditure					
Fundraising and Publicity		-	2,562	2,562	1,893
Shop operating costs		-	5,047	5,047	4,173
Management and Administration		1,250	8,827	10,077	7,372
Total Resources Expended	6	138,558	107,231	245,789	191,943

➤ *CONTINUED*

Net Incoming Resources for the Year is the result of subtracting the resources expended from the incoming resources. It is not an operating surplus, however, as it includes the surplus funds on the donation for the purchase of fixed assets. This would have been excluded from the surplus on an income and expenditure account, as it would have been treated as deferred income. The net incoming resources for the year can also include specific grants and donations which have to be carried forward until they can be spent on the specific purpose. Where there are incoming endowment funds, then the net incoming resources will also include those for the year. There is also an element of the net incoming resources for the year which will represent the surplus or deficit for the year. Further explanation on this is given in note 12. Charities can choose to explain the figure on net incoming resources, if they consider that this may be misunderstood by readers of the accounts.

Other Recognised Gains and Losses will show the movements due to revaluations or sales of fixed assets and investments. In this case, there is just the change in the market value of the investments, which is a gain. It is an unrealised gain, because the investment has not been sold, it is simply worth more on paper.

Net Movement in Funds shows the overall surplus or deficit in each fund for the year.

Funds at 1 April 1996 shows the balances brought forward from the end of the previous financial year. These should agree to the balances on the Balance Sheet for the previous year. When adopting this format of accounts for the first year, calculations will have to be made to get to these opening balances.

Funds at 31 March 1997 is calculated by adding the net movement in funds to the funds brought forward. These amounts represent the balance in each fund, but not necessarily the amount of free reserves. The reader is referred to note 13 as this explains the analysis of the funds into assets and liabilities.

Movements on reserves... – The final sentence reflects the requirements of Financial Reporting Standard 3 (FRS 3), which requires certain information to be disclosed in accounts. Note that the SOFA includes the information which would go into a "Statement of Recognised Gains and Losses". This can be shown in a different layout, as demonstrated in the alternative layout at the end of these accounts.

Charities may choose to add the statement *"The notes on pages xx to xx form part of these accounts"*. This helps to draw the reader's attention to the notes.

➤ *CONTINUED*

Net Incoming Resources for the Year		17,207	8,669	25,876	40,723
Other Recognised Gains and Losses					
Unrealised Gain on Investments	8	–	762	762	202
Net Movement in Funds		17,207	9,431	26,638	40,925
Funds at 1 April 1996		1,316	25,594	26,910	(14,015)
Funds at 31 March 1997	13	18,523	35,025	53,548	26,910

Movements on reserves and all recognised gains and losses are shown above.

Explanatory Notes
Summary Income and Expenditure Account

This charity is incorporated as a company and the Companies Acts do not allow unrealised gains to be shown in an income and expenditure account. The SORP requires the gain on revaluation of investments to be shown in the SOFA, so in this case the SOFA cannot comply with both the SORP and the Companies Acts. A separate statement has to be prepared to show the simple income and expenditure of the charity, but it does not need to be separated into restricted and unrestricted funds.

This may not be required for unincorporated charities, who may adapt the layout of the SOFA to incorporate both an income and expenditure account and the statement of total recognised gains and losses on one page, as demonstrated in the alternative layout at the end of these accounts. Note that the summary income and expenditure account will be needed for all charities with movments on endowment funds.

ELDERLY CONCERN CAMBERWICK
SUMMARY INCOME AND EXPENDITURE ACCOUNT
For the year ended 31 March 1997

	1997 £	1996 £
Total income of continuing operations	271,665	232,666
Total expenditure of continuing operations	245,789	191,943
Net income for the year	25,876	40,723

Explanatory Notes
Balance Sheet

This example shows the total balance sheet figures, with the details given in the notes to the accounts. More detail can be given on the face of the balance sheet. In particular, the analysis of assets and liabilities into restricted and unrestricted funds can be given in a columnar format, similar to the SOFA, if preferred. An example of this layout is given in Chapter 5.

Fixed Assets must be divided between tangible fixed assets and investments, including investment properties.

Tangible fixed assets are equipment, property and any other physical items used for the functioning of the charity. The balance sheet shows the net book value and further details must be given in the notes.

Investments must be stated at market value and so must be revalued at the balance sheet date (SORP requirement). Investments should be shown under fixed assets where there is an intention to keep the assets for some time. If the investments are short-term holdings, then these would appear under current assets.

Debtors are the amounts due to the charity at the balance sheet date and should all be recoverable. Provision should be made for any bad debts.

Cash at Bank and in Hand includes all bank accounts, deposit and current, as well as the balance in the petty cash at the balance sheet date.

Creditors: Amounts Falling Due Within One Year are the current liabilities of the charity.

Net Current Assets are calculated as the difference between the total current assets and the creditors falling due within one year.

Net Assets totals the fixed assets and the net current assets. This figure should always be the same as the total funds of the charity.

Funds is the part of the balance sheet which summarises all the balances of the funds. More detail can be given on the face of the balance sheet, for example the analysis of the restricted funds, or this information can be given in the notes to the accounts as here. The figures here should agree to the bottom line on the SOFA. Additional information is also given here as the balance sheet separates out the designated funds and the accumulated revaluation gains, which are not shown on the SOFA. The revaluation fund is shown separately because the Companies Act requires separate disclosure of revaluation reserves on the face of the balance sheet. These are the unrealised gains on the investments, being the difference between the original price paid and the market value at the balance sheet date.

These financial statements were approved by... – the accounts, together with the notes, are collectively called financial statements and must be approved at a meeting of the trustees. At least one trustee signs the balance sheet on behalf of all trustees.

ELDERLY CONCERN CAMBERWICK
(A company limited by guarantee)
BALANCE SHEET
As at 31 March 1997

	Notes	1997 £	1997 £	1996 £
Fixed Assets				
Tangible Fixed Assets	7		11,250	10,000
Investments	8		11,654	10,892
			22,904	20,892
Current Assets				
Debtors	9	7,835		5,628
Cash at Bank and in Hand		31,193		9,142
		39,028		14,770
Creditors: Amounts Falling Due Within One Year	10	8,384		8,752
Net Current Assets			30,644	6,018
Net Assets			53,548	26,910
Funds				
Unrestricted Funds:				
General Funds			23,196	24,527
Revaluation Fund			1,829	1,067
Designated Funds	11		10,000	–
			35,025	25,594
Restricted Funds	12		18,523	1,316
Total Funds	13		53,548	26,910

These financial statements were approved by the Directors
on 13 September 1997 and signed on their behalf by

....
P Farthing – Treasurer

Explanatory Notes
Notes to the Accounts

Accounting policies must be described for all relevant matters.

a) It is taken for granted that the accounts are prepared on the accruals basis and follow other fundamental accounting concepts. The reference to applicable accounting standards confirms this, however, but also confirms compliance with many other standards. The auditor or independent examiner has to check that the accounts do comply with these standards.

There should also be a statement that the SORP is being followed. For clarification, the date of the final version of the SORP has been included.

b) **Voluntary income** – confirmation that all donations and gifts are included in the SOFA when received.

c) **Grants** – need to explain the basis for inclusion. A statement similar to the one for voluntary income may be sufficient, but consider whether there are any particular circumstances or policies. The example explains the treatment of grants for the purchase of fixed assets.

d) **Restricted funds** will need an accounting policy to explain how the charity identifies such funds.

e) **Unrestricted funds** need to be explained as appropriate, clarifying any terminology used by the charity.

f) **Designated funds policy** should describe the principle underlying designated funds, not a detailed breakdown of the particular funds, which should be given elsewhere.

g) **Staff costs and overheads** need to be allocated and apportioned on some consistent basis from year to year. The accounting policy given in these notes needs to describe adequately the methodology, without so much detail that it would be inaccurate or have to be changed every year.

h) **Fundraising and publicity costs** should be explained to give an understanding of how this category applies to this charity.

i) **Management and administration costs** – the basis for identifying these in this particular charity.

j) **Depreciation rates** for each class of asset should be given, or the estimated useful life of each class of asset.

k) **Investments** – the fact that these are revalued at the balance sheet date as required by the SORP needs to be stated as a policy. Further policy notes may be required if different classes of investments are held as both fixed assets and as short-term investments. It is not necessary to explain the trustees' investment policy here; that type of explanation would belong in the Annual Report.

Further accounting policies are required by some other accounting standards if they apply to the charity, for example if they have operating leases. Further policies should be explained if necessary.

ELDERLY CONCERN CAMBERWICK
NOTES TO THE ACCOUNTS
For the year ended 31 March 1997

1. Accounting Policies

a) The financial statements have been prepared in accordance with applicable accounting standards and follow the recommendations in Statement of Recommended Practice: Accounting by Charities (SORP) issued October 1995.

b) Voluntary income is received by way of donations and gifts and is included in full in the Statement of Financial Activities when received.

c) Grants including grants for the purchase of fixed assets are recognised in full in the Statement of Financial Activities in the year in which they are received.

d) Restricted funds are to be used for specified purposes as laid down by the donor. Expenditure which meets these criteria is identified to the fund, together with a fair allocation of management and support costs.

e) Unrestricted funds are donations and other income received or generated for the objects of the charity without further specified purpose and are available as general funds.

f) Designated funds are unrestricted funds earmarked by the trustees for particular purposes.

g) Staff costs and overhead expenses are allocated to activities on the basis of staff time spent on those activities.

h) Fundraising and publicity costs comprise the costs actually incurred in producing materials for promotional purposes, and of raising funds through the charity shop.

i) Management and administration costs of the charity relate to the costs of running the charity such as the costs of meetings, audit and statutory compliance, and includes any costs which cannot be specifically identified to another expenditure classification.

j) Depreciation is provided on all tangible fixed assets at rates calculated to write off the cost of each asset over its estimated useful life, which in all cases is set at four years.

k) Investments held as fixed assets are revalued at mid-market value at the balance sheet date and the gain or loss taken to the Statement of Financial Activities.

➤ *CONTINUED*

Note 2 – Grants

This note gives further information on the source of grants and their purpose. Further information may be added if required by the funders, such as an explanation of the application of funds.

Note 3 – Donations

Further information on the source of significant donations is given, splitting them between restricted and unrestricted.

Note 4 – Staff Costs and Numbers

The Companies Acts require staff costs to be analysed into gross salary and employer's national insurance contributions (social security costs). If there are other pension contributions or other benefits, these should also be given in the note. The SORP requires the total emoluments of all staff to be given, including all benefits in kind as computed for tax purposes. Since some benefits to staff are not charged to staff costs in the expenditure classification, and not necessarily assessed on the basis of cost, the note may not agree to the amount charged to staff costs elsewhere in the accounts. For example, some staff may have charity cars, which are assessed by the Inland Revenue as a taxable benefit, but not on the basis of the actual cost to the charity. The cost of cars would appear elsewhere in the accounts. The note will have to be adapted to add the extra information required by the SORP.

The number of staff employed needs to be given as an average for the year, analysed into appropriate categories of activities.

Note 5 – Trustees' Remuneration and Expenses

A note must be included even if the amounts of both remuneration and expenses are nil. There is no need to detail who received the expenses, but the total paid out and the nature of the expenses should be stated. Trustees should not be remunerated unless special consent has been given by the Charity Commission and it is permitted under the governing instrument.

➤ *CONTINUED*

ELDERLY CONCERN CAMBERWICK
NOTES TO THE ACCOUNTS
For the year ended 31 March 1997

	1997 £	1996 £
2. Grants		
Borough of Camberwick: Advice and Advocacy	70,000	60,000
Wickshire County Council: Domiciliary Care	80,000	66,132
	150,000	126,132
3. Donations		
Restricted		
Camberwick Charitable Trust -		
for the purchase of computer equipment	5,000	–
Unrestricted		
For the general purposes of the charity	–	6,796
	5,000	6,796
4. Staff Costs and Numbers		
Staff costs during the year were as follows:		
Salaries and Wages	191,769	144,247
Social Security Costs	19,560	15,364
	211,329	159,611
Total emoluments paid to staff were	191,769	144,247

The average number of employees (part-time and full-time) during the year was as follows:

Chief Officer	1
Advice and Advocacy	4
Domiciliary Care	4
Luncheon Club	6
Administration and Support	1
	16

5. Trustees' Remuneration and Expenses

The trustees received no remuneration. Five trustees were reimbursed expenses as follows:

	1997 £	1996 £
Travel Expenses	137	164
Reimbursement of postage and stationery	29	20
	166	184

Note 6 – Total Resources Expended

There is no set format for this note, but the example complies with the recommendation that the natural classification of expenditure should be given as well as the activity based classification in the SOFA. This format also gives a reader sufficient understanding of the component elements of each expenditure heading. A lot of the expenditure headings have been allocated across several cost centres; the basis will need to be followed consistently.

ELDERLY CONCERN CAMBERWICK
NOTES TO THE ACCOUNTS
For the year ended 31 March 1997

6. Total Resources Expended

	Advice and Advocacy £	Domiciliary Care £	Luncheon Club £	Fundraising and Publicity £	Shop Operating Costs £	Mgmt and Admin £	1997 Total £	1996 Total £
Staff Costs	64,239	60,568	84,644	–	–	1,878	211,329	159,611
Recruitment	–	1,426	1,212	–	–	–	2,638	5,557
Travel	324	482	396	–	–	166	1,368	1,038
Premises	1,646	3,931	2,019	–	3,065	–	10,661	10,562
Communications	594	589	1,274	–	459	589	3,505	2,816
Legal and Professional	–	–	–	–	–	1,250	1,250	2,870
Audit and Accountancy	–	–	–	–	–	2,000	2,000	1,800
Consultancy	–	770	–	–	–	2,336	3,106	–
Annual Report	–	–	–	2,562	–	–	2,562	1,893
Volunteer Expenses	1,489	–	–	–	1,523	–	3,012	2,844
Depreciation	625	625	1,250	–	–	1,250	3,750	2,500
Bank Charges	–	–	–	–	–	608	608	452
	68,917	68,391	90,795	2,562	5,047	10,077	245,789	191,943

Note 7 – Tangible Fixed Assets

There is only one category of fixed assets in this example. It is necessary to show separately assets which are very different in nature, so freehold land and buildings, leasehold land and buildings, equipment and motor vehicles would be in separate categories. Cost, depreciation and net book value should be shown as brought forward figures, change in year and carried forward figure. In this example, the additions in the year are the purchase of computer equipment funded by the specific donation described in Note 3.

Note 8 – Investments

Investments have to be revalued at market value at each balance sheet date and the gain or loss taken to the SOFA. The original or historical cost also has to be shown in the note to the accounts. Different types of investments should be shown separately in the note, such as listed UK shares, listed overseas shares, unquoted companies, property, investments in common investment funds, cash, and other investments. Charities with significant investment portfolios should describe these in more detail and explain their investment policies in the trustees' annual report.

Note 9 – Debtors

Any breakdown of the debtors total shown on the balance sheet which will help a reader to understand the nature of the amounts due should be given. The minimum required is an analysis into:

◆ trade debtors

◆ amounts owed by connected bodies

◆ other debtors

◆ prepayments

Note 10 – Creditors

It is a requirement to show separately in this note:

◆ loans and overdrafts

◆ trade creditors

◆ amounts due to any connected body

◆ other creditors

◆ accruals and deferred income

Headings may be omitted where there is nothing to state against them.

ELDERLY CONCERN CAMBERWICK
NOTES TO THE ACCOUNTS
For the year ended 31 March 1997

7. Tangible Fixed Assets

	Office Equipment £
COST	
At 1 April 1996	15,000
Additions	5,000
At 31 March 1997	20,000
DEPRECIATION	
At 1 April 1996	5,000
Charge for Year	3,750
At 31 March 1997	8,750
NET BOOK VALUE	
At 31 March 1997	**11,250**
At 31 March 1996	**10,000**

8. Investments

	1997 £	1996 £
Charifund Unit Trust shares at mid-market value:		
At 1 April 1996	10,892	10,690
Change in value	762	202
At 31 March 1997	**11,654**	**10,892**
Historical cost of investments held at 31 March 1997	9,825	9,825

9. Debtors

Contract Fees Receivable	6,709	4,580
Other Debtors and Prepayments	1,126	1,048
	7,835	**5,628**

10. Creditors: Amounts Falling Due Within One Year

Taxation and Social Security	4,458	3,896
Other Creditors and Accruals	3,926	4,856
	8,384	**8,752**

Note 11 – Designated Funds

The purpose of the designation(s) should be made clear as well as movements in the fund balances in the year.

Note 12 – Restricted Funds

The note needs to explain what the total balance carried forward in the balance sheet relates to. It is helpful to identify how the restricted fund will be used in the future.

Note 13 – Analysis of Net Assets Between Funds

The assets and liabilities of the charity must be identified to the particular fund. This can be done by adopting a columnar format for the Balance Sheet, but can be done by a note in this format. Where there has been a revaluation, it is a requirement of the Companies Acts that the amount of the reserves attributable to the revaluation should be shown. This information is shown here, but is also shown on the face of the balance sheet. The information does not have to be repeated and could be omitted here.

ELDERLY CONCERN CAMBERWICK
NOTES TO THE ACCOUNTS
For the year ended 31 March 1997

11. Designated Funds

The trustees have designated funds for purchase
of new equipment in the luncheon club.

	£
Transferred in Year and at 31 March 1997	10,000

12. Restricted Funds

The movements on the restricted funds of the charity were as follows:

	1 April 1996 £	Incoming £	Outgoing £	31 March 1997 £
a) Computer Equipment	–	5,000	1,250	3,750
b) Advice and Advocacy	1,316	70,000	68,917	2,399
c) Domiciliary Care	–	80,765	68,391	12,374
	1,316	155,765	138,558	18,523

The balances will be carried forward and used as follows:
- a) The balance will fund future depreciation charges
- b) The balance will be used to continue the advice and advocacy activity with the terms of the fund
- c) The balance arose from a delay in appointing new staff and will all be utilised in the forthcoming months.

13. Analysis of Net Assets Between Funds

	Restricted Funds £	Unrestricted Funds £	Total Funds £
Fund Balances at 31 March 1997 are represented by:			
Tangible Fixed Assets	3,750	7,500	11,250
Investments	–	11,654	11,654
Current Assets	17,229	21,799	39,028
Creditors: Amounts Falling Due Within One Year	(2,456)	(5,928)	(8,384)
Total Net Assets	18,523	35,025	53,548
Unrealised gains included above on investments	–	1,829	1,829

Explanatory Notes
Alternative Layout for an Unincorporated Charity

The SOFA has been split into two sections.

The first section is labelled Income and Expenditure and ends with Net Income for the Year. This is a statement of the income and expenditure relating to revenue transactions.

The second section is labelled Statement of Total Recognised Gains and Losses. It brings in the net income and then adds the unrealised gain to get to the sub-total, described as the Net Movement on Funds. This is then reconciled to funds brought forward and funds carried forward.

This layout will comply with the requirements of FRS 3 and then there is no need to produce the summary income and expenditure account in addition to the SOFA.

Alternative Layout for an Unincorporated Charity
UNINCORPORATED ELDERLY CONCERN
STATEMENT OF FINANCIAL ACTIVITIES
For the year ended 31 March 1997

Notes		Restricted £	Unrestricted £	Total £	1996 £
Income and Expenditure					
Incoming Resources					
Grants	2	150,000	–	150,000	126,132
Local Authority Contracts		–	95,000	95,000	80,414
Donations	3	5,000	–	5,000	6,796
Charity shop – donated goods		–	20,000	20,000	18,000
Investment Income		765	900	1,665	1,324
Total Incoming Resources		155,765	115,900	271,665	232,666
Resources Expended					
Direct Charitable Expenditure					
Advice and Advocacy		68,917	–	68,917	61,756
Domiciliary Care		68,391	–	68,391	53,316
Luncheon Club		–	90,795	90,795	63,433
		137,308	90,795	228,103	178,505
Other Expenditure					
Fundraising and Publicity		–	2,562	2,562	1,893
Shop operating costs		–	5,047	5,047	4,173
Management and Administration		1,250	8,827	10,077	7,372
Total Resources Expended	6	138,558	107,231	245,789	191,943
Net Income for the Year		17,207	8,669	25,876	40,723
Statement of Total Recognised Gains and Losses					
Net Income for the year		17,207	8,669	25,876	40,723
Unrealised Gain on Investments	8	–	762	762	202
Net Movement in Funds		17,207	9,431	26,638	40,925
Funds at 1 April 1996		1,316	25,594	26,910	(14,015)
Funds at 31 March 1997	13	18,523	35,025	53,548	26,910

Movements on reserves and all recognised gains and losses are shown above.
All of the charity's operations are classed as continuing.

Chapter 7

LARGER CHARITY

This chapter includes an example set of accounts for a fairly large charity with more complex operations. It is representative of a large number of local and national charities. It has gross income of just over £1 million and net assets of nearly £300,000. It provides services, which it funds from a combination of fees, grants and donations. It has a small trading subsidiary, but no endowment funds.

Content of Accounts

A set of accounts or financial statements should consist of the following:

- Annual Report of the Trustees (Directors' Report)
- Statement of Financial Activities
- Summary Income and Expenditure Account (for some charities)
- Balance Sheet
- Cashflow Statement (only a requirement for large organisations)
- Notes to the Accounts
- Auditor's Report

The annual report for this organisation is not given here and the auditor's report would follow the example in Chapter 8 for a charitable company. Otherwise full accounts are given, including the cashflow statement.

Example Accounts

The example in this chapter illustrates the treatment for a number of matters:

- ◆ charitable company
- ◆ consolidated accounts for main charity and its trading subsidiary
- ◆ deferred income on SOFA
- ◆ grants for the purchase of fixed assets
- ◆ service providing charity with both restricted and unrestricted funding for some projects
- ◆ transfer of unrestricted funds to represent "top-up" to a project mainly dealt with in unrestricted funds
- ◆ revaluation of property used for charitable purposes

Explanatory Notes
Consolidated Statement of Financial Activities (SOFA)

The transactions for the charity and its trading subsidiary are added together to produce the consolidated SOFA. It is still split into restricted and unrestricted funds; the net income from the subsidiary is brought in as unrestricted funds.

Comparative figures should be shown for the preceding year; these do not have to be analysed into restricted and unrestricted funds.

Grants are explained in more detail in note 2. There is a grant of £20,000 which specifically relates to the following financial year, so this is deferred. Note the disclosure of the deferral is required on the face of the SOFA. The deferred grant will also be included in creditors.

Net income of trading subsidiary is the net profits of the subsidiary. If the subsidiary undertakes non-charitable trading, then it is appropriate to include the net profit under incoming resources, according to the SORP. If the subsidiary was undertaking charitable activities, then the consolidation should be done on a "line-by-line" basis, i.e. including the gross figures in with the appropriate income or expenditure. The consolidation should eliminate inter-company transactions, such as the receipt by the charity of donations from the trading subsidiary. This line of income is replaced by the net profit of the subsidiary, so effectively it includes profits whether or not they have been transferred to the charity.

Charges to residents are unrestricted income as these are the fees to the residents or the authorities responsible for them. This is charitable trading income and could be classified as such.

Direct Charitable Expenditure is further broken down into the main areas of activity for this charity. This includes **support costs** in this example.

Fundraising and Publicity – If there is no expenditure on fundraising and publicity, then this heading may be omitted. Fundraising costs could be allocated to both restricted and unrestricted funds, depending on the nature of the restricted funds and the type of fundraising. For example, the restriction may exist because the funds may only be used in a particular geographical area, but they were raised from an appeal, the costs of which can be identified.

Management and Administration will be a heading for nearly every charity and will usually be part of the unrestricted funds.

Total Resources Expended – A note to the accounts should give the analysis of expenditure into the natural headings, and the note number by Total Resources Expended refers the reader to this note.

Net Incoming Resources Before Transfers is the result of subtracting the resources expended from the incoming resources. The net incoming resources for the year can be a straightforward surplus or deficit, but will also include specific grants and donations which have to be carried forward until they can be spent on the specific purpose.

CAMBERWICK SERVICES FOR THE MENTALLY ILL
CONSOLIDATED STATEMENT OF FINANCIAL ACTIVITIES
For the year ended 31 March 1997

	Notes	Unrestricted £	Restricted £	Total £	1996 £
Incoming Resources					
Grants		777,858	172,766	950,624	851,125
less: Grants Deferred		(20,000)	(-)	(20,000)	(40,000)
	2	757,858	172,766	930,624	811,125
Donations		2,000	3,000	5,000	5,675
Charges to Residents		–	365,980	365,980	353,651
Net Income of Trading Subsidiary	10	–	15,150	15,150	17,134
Interest Receivable		–	2,098	2,098	4,402
Net Gain on Disposal of Fixed Assets		–	9,333	9,333	–
Other Income		–	9,101	9,101	7,975
Total Incoming Resources		759,858	577,428	1,337,286	1,199,962
Resources Expended					
Direct Charitable Expenditure					
Residential Services		389,933	352,833	742,766	714,858
Day Care		256,305	–	256,305	210,991
Other Projects		62,018	79,769	141,787	70,169
Support Costs		34,010	74,462	108,472	100,494
		742,266	507,064	1,249,330	1,096,512
Other Expenditure					
Fundraising and Publicity		–	22,050	22,050	20,487
Management and Administration		–	14,512	14,512	12,246
Total Resources Expended	3	742,266	543,626	1,285,892	1,129,245
Net Incoming Resources Before Transfers	4	17,592	33,802	51,394	70,717

➤ CONTNUED

Transfers Between Funds is a transfer from unrestricted to restricted. If a project which is defined as restricted (because it is or has been wholly or mainly funded by restricted income) has a shortfall of funding in a particular year, then a transfer can be made from unrestricted funds to support the activity. There will be occasions where funds are transferred from restricted funds to unrestricted funds, but it will be necessary to obtain the permission of the donor and possibly the Charity Commission. Sometimes it will be in the terms of the gift that the transfer may be made, e.g. of interest income arising on the gift.

Other Recognised Gains and Losses will show the movements due to revaluations or sales of fixed assets and investments. In this case, there was a revaluation of the property in the previous financial year.

Net Movement in Funds shows the overall surplus or deficit in each fund for the year.

Funds at 1 April 1996 shows the balances brought forward from the end of the previous financial year. These should agree to the balances on the Balance Sheet for the previous year. When adopting this format of accounts for the first year, calculations will have to be made to get to these opening balances.

Funds at 31 March 1997 is calculated by adding the net movement in funds to the funds brought forward. These amounts represent the balance in each fund, but not necessarily the amount of free reserves. The reader is referred to note 15 as this explains the analysis of the funds into assets and liabilities.

All of the group's... – The final sentences reflect the requirements of Financial Reporting Standard 3 (FRS 3), which requires certain information to be disclosed in accounts. Note that the SOFA includes the information which would go into a "Statement of Recognised Gains and Losses".

> CONTINUED

CAMBERWICK SERVICES FOR THE MENTALLY ILL
CONSOLIDATED STATEMENT OF FINANCIAL ACTIVITIES
For the year ended 31 March 1997

	Notes	Restricted £	Unrestricted £	Total £	1996 £
Transfer Between Funds	5	19,000	(19,000)	–	–
Net Incoming Resources For the Year		36,592	14,802	51,394	70,717
Other Recognised Gains and Losses					
Unrealised Gain on Tangible Fixed Asset		–	–	–	134,835
Net Movement on Funds		36,592	14,802	51,394	205,552
Funds at 1 April 1996		10,865	237,210	248,075	42,523
Funds at 31 March 1997	15	**47,457**	**252,012**	**299,469**	**248,075**

All of the group's activities are classed as continuing. Movements on reserves and all recognised gains and losses are shown above.

Explanatory Notes
Summary Income and Expenditure Account

This charity is incorporated as a company and the Companies Acts do not allow unrealised gains to be shown in an income and expenditure account. The SORP requires the gain on revaluation of fixed assets to be shown in the SOFA, so in this case the SOFA cannot comply with both the SORP and the Companies Acts. A separate statement has to be prepared to show the simple income and expenditure of the charity, but it does not need to be separated into restricted and unrestricted funds. If there are no further revaluations next year, then the summary income and expenditure account will not be required, unless the charity receives incoming resources to an endowment fund.

The summary income and expenditure account describes income and expenditure for continuing activities. FRS 3 requires organisations to split the income and expenditure into continuing, discontinued and acquired activities. This will rarely apply to charities, as they do not often buy and sell whole businesses. A charity would only have to undertake this split if it changed its activities in a significant way; the closing of a project will not usually constitute a "discontinued" activity. If it were necessary, then this split could be given in the summary income and expenditure account and the SOFA would remain unchanged.

CAMBERWICK SERVICES FOR THE MENTALLY ILL
CONSOLIDATED SUMMARY INCOME AND EXPENDITURE ACCOUNT
For the year ended 31 March 1997

	1995 £	1996 £
Gross Income of Continuing Operations	1,312,803	1,182,828
Non-charitable Trading Activities: Net Income	15,150	17,134
Total Income of Continuing Operations	1,327,953	1,199,962
Total Expenditure of Continuing Operations	1,285,892	1,129,245
Net Income before Asset Disposals	42,061	70,717
Gain on Disposal of Fixed Assets	9,333	-
Net Income for the Year	51,394	70,717

Explanatory Notes
Balance Sheet

This example shows the balance sheet for both the charity and its subsidiary together ("group") and for the charity on its own ("charity") This columnar format is conventional for groups of companies. All the details concerning the analysis of assets and liabilities into restricted and unrestricted funds are given in the notes to the accounts.

Fixed Assets must be divided between tangible fixed assets and investments.

Tangible fixed assets are equipment, property and any other physical items. The balance sheet shows the net book value and further details must be given in the notes.

Investments in this example only apply to the parent company, the charity. It has shares in the trading subsidiary which cost £100. Their value would be difficult to determine, but this is largely the reason why additional information is given concerning the results of the trading subsidiary in the notes to the accounts. Since it is likely that most of the profits are transferred to the charity, then the trading subsidiary would have very little value to anyone else and its worth is not likely to be greater than its net assets. It may be necessary to write down the value of the investments if the trading subsidiary was making losses. The investment of £100 is only shown in the charity balance sheet. On consolidation, this is replaced in the group balance sheet with the net assets of the subsidiary.

Stock is held in the trading subsidiary, but not in the charity. Hence it is shown in the group balance sheet, but not in the charity balance sheet.

Debtors are the amounts due to the charity at the balance sheet date and should all be recoverable. Provision should be made for any bad debts.

Cash at Bank and in Hand includes all bank accounts, deposit and current, as well as the balance in the petty cash at the balance sheet date.

Creditors: Amounts Falling Due Within One Year are the current liabilities of the group and charity. This will include the deferred grants from the SOFA.

Net Current Assets are calculated as the difference between the total current assets and the creditors falling due within one year.

Creditors: Amounts Falling Due After One Year are the long term liabilities of the charity. In this example, the charity has a loan which is being repaid in instalments of £10,000 per annum. There are two instalments left to repay, so £10,000 is shown as due within one year and £10,000 as due after one year.

Net Assets totals the fixed assets, the net current assets and the long term liabilities. This figure should always be the same as the total funds of the group and charity.

Funds is the part of the balance sheet which summarises all the balances of the funds. The figures here should agree to the bottom line on the SOFA.

Approved by…- the accounts must be approved at a meeting of the trustees. At least one trustee signs the balance sheet on behalf of all trustees.

CAMBERWICK SERVICES FOR THE MENTALLY ILL
(A company limited by guarantee)
BALANCE SHEET
As at 31 March 1997

	Notes	The Group 1997 £	The Group 1996 £	The Charity 1997 £	The Charity 1996 £
Fixed Assets					
Tangible Fixed Assets	9	211,952	207,674	211,952	207,674
Investments	10	–	–	100	100
		211,952	207,674	212,052	207,774
Current Assets					
Stock	11	2,162	1,854	–	–
Debtors	12	39,015	42,875	44,431	47,250
Cash at Bank and in Hand		246,566	191,177	231,666	180,207
		287,743	235,906	276,097	227,457
Creditors: Amounts Falling Due Within One Year	13	(190,226)	(175,505)	(185,111)	(171,437)
Net Current Assets		97,517	60,401	90,986	56,020
Total Assets Less Current Liabilities		309,469	268,075	303,038	263,794
Creditors: Amounts Falling Due After One Year	14	(10,000)	(20,000)	(10,000)	(20,000)
Net Assets	15	299,469	248,075	293,038	243,794
Funds					
Restricted Funds	16	47,457	10,865	47,457	10,865
Unrestricted Funds: General Fund		117,177	102,375	110,746	98,094
Revaluation Fund		134,835	134,835	134,835	134,835
Total Funds		299,469	248,075	293,038	243,794

Approved by the Directors on 17 July 1997 and signed on their behalf by

.... A Director

Explanatory Notes
Consolidated Cashflow Statement

A cashflow statement is only required for larger charities and is not compulsory for this charity. It is included here to provide an example. The size criteria are set out for companies, but will apply to all charities, whether incorporated or not. A "small" organisation will meet two of the following criteria:

◆ gross income less than £2.8 million

◆ net assets less than £1.4 million

◆ less than 50 employees

If the organisation exceeds the size criteria above for the current or preceding year, then a cashflow statement must be prepared.

CAMBERWICK SERVICES FOR THE MENTALLY ILL
CONSOLIDATED CASHFLOW STATEMENT
For the year ended 31 March 1997

		1997	1996
	£	£	£
Net Cash Inflow from Operating Activities		67,075	80,065
Investing Activities			
Purchase of Tangible Fixed Assets	(25,430)		(5,230)
Proceeds from Sale of Tangible Fixed Assets	13,744		–
Net Cash Outflow from Investing Activities		(11,686)	(5,230)
Increase in Cash and Cash Equivalents		55,389	74,835
Cash and Cash Equivalents at 31 March 1996		191,177	124,342
Cash and Cash Equivalents at 31 March 1997		246,566	199,177

Notes to the Cashflow Statement

	£	£
1. *Reconciliation of Changes in Resources to Net Cash Inflow from Operating Activities*		
Changes in resources before revaluations	51,394	70,717
Depreciation	16,741	14,343
Gain on disposal of tangible fixed assets	(9,333)	–
Increase in creditors: current liabilities	14,721	4,391
Decrease in creditors: long term	(10,000)	(10,000)
Decrease in debtors	3,860	1,043
Increase in stock	(308)	(429)
	67,075	80,065

2. *Analysis of Changes in Cash and Cash Equivalents During the Year*

	1997	1996	Change in Year
	£	£	£
Cash at bank and in hand	**246,566**	**191,177**	**55,389**

Explanatory Notes
Notes to the Accounts

Accounting policies must be described for all relevant matters.

a) It is taken for granted that the accounts are prepared on the accruals basis and follow other fundamental accounting concepts. The reference to applicable accounting standards confirms this, however, but also confirms compliance with many other standards. The auditor or independent examiner has to check that the accounts do comply with these standards.

There should also be a statement that the SORP is being followed.

In addition, there is an explanation of the basis of the group accounts and the method of consolidation. As there is only a SOFA on a consolidated basis, this is also explained here.

b) Voluntary income – confirmation that all donations and gifts are included in the SOFA when received. The basis for inclusion of intangible income and gifts in kind is also covered.

c) Revenue Grants – need to explain the basis for inclusion. The example explains that grants may need to be deferred if they relate to a future period.

d) Grants for the purchase of fixed assets are explained in a separate accounting policy. The link to the depreciation charge in the SOFA is explained. An explanation of any change in the accounting policy will have to be given, as well as an explanation of any prior year adjustment arising from the change in policy.

e) Restricted funds will need an accounting policy to explain how the charity identifies such funds.

f) Unrestricted funds need to be explained as appropriate, clarifying any terminology used by the charity.

g) Designated funds policy should describe the principle underlying designated funds, not a detailed breakdown of the particular funds, which should be given elsewhere.

h) Staff costs and overheads need to be allocated and apportioned on some consistent basis from year to year. The accounting policy given in these notes needs to describe adequately the methodology, without so much detail that it would be inaccurate or have to be changed every year.

i) Depreciation rates for each class of asset should be given, or the estimated useful life of each class of asset. Property should be depreciated unless the residual value will exceed the net book value shown in the balance sheet or if the organisation maintains the property to a standard which ensures that the market value could be obtained when sold. This charity has revalued its freehold property and maintains it adequately, so has a policy of not depreciating the property.

CAMBERWICK SERVICES FOR THE MENTALLY ILL
NOTES TO THE ACCOUNTS
For the year ended 31 March 1997

1. **Accounting Policies**

    a) The financial statements have been prepared in accordance with applicable accounting standards and follow the recommendations in Statement of Recommended Practice: Accounting by Charities.

    Consolidated financial statements ("group accounts") have been prepared in respect of the charitable company ("charity") and its wholly owned subsidiary, Trading Company Limited. The results of Trading Company Limited have been consolidated into the Statement of Financial Activities on the basis of the net profit before transfers to Camberwick Services for the Mentally Ill. In accordance with Section 230 of the Companies Act 1985, a separate Statement of Financial Activities for Camberwick Services for the Mentally Ill has not been presented.

    b) Voluntary income received by way of donations and gifts to the charity is included in full in the Statement of Financial Activities when received. Intangible income is not included unless it represents goods or services which would have otherwise been purchased. Gifts in kind are valued and brought in as income and the appropriate expenditure.

    c) Revenue grants are credited to incoming resources on the earlier date of when they are received or when they are receivable, unless they relate to a specified future period, in which case they are deferred.

    d) Grants for the purchase of fixed assets are credited to restricted incoming resources when receivable. Depreciation on the fixed assets purchased with such grants is charged against the restricted fund.

    e) Restricted funds are to be used for specified purposes as laid down by the donor. Expenditure which meets these criteria is identified to the fund, together with a fair allocation of overheads and support costs.

    f) Unrestricted funds are donations and other incoming resources received or generated for the charitable purposes.

    g) Designated funds are unrestricted funds earmarked by the directors for particular purposes.

    h) Staff costs and overhead expenses are allocated to activities on the basis of staff time spent on those activities.

    i) Depreciation is provided on tangible fixed assets at rates calculated to write off the cost of each asset over its expected useful life, which is set at four years for motor vehicles and furniture and equipment. No depreciation is provided on freehold buildings, since they are maintained to a standard at which the market value could be realised.

j) Stocks – the basis of the valuation of stocks at the balance sheet date should be given. It is usual to state that it is the lower of cost or net realisable value, which is the basis required by Statement of Standard Accounting Practice 9 (SSAP 9). Donated goods held for resale are not valued when held as stock.

k) Rentals payable under operating leases should be treated as an ordinary expenditure item. This policy is a requirement of SSAP 21. If the charity has finance leases, then the policy note would have to be expanded accordingly.

l) Where the charity operates a pension scheme the type of pension should be identified, i.e. whether it is defined contribution or defined benefit. The liabilities to the charity should then be identified accordingly.

Note 2 – Grants

This note gives further information on the source of grants and the movement on the deferral of grants brought forward and carried forward. Further information may be added if required by the funders.

CAMBERWICK SERVICES FOR THE MENTALLY ILL
NOTES TO THE ACCOUNTS
For the year ended 31 March 1997

1. **Accounting Policies** (continued)

j) Stocks of purchased goods are valued at the lower of cost and net realisable value. Stocks of donated goods are not valued for accounting purposes.

k) Rentals payable under operating leases, where substantially all the risks and rewards of ownership remain with the lessor, are charged to the Statement of Financial Activities in the year in which they fall due.

l) The charity operates a defined contribution pension scheme.The assets of the scheme are held separately from those of the charity in an independently administered fund.The pension cost charge represents the contributions payable under the scheme by the charity to the fund. The charity has no liability under the scheme other than for the payment of those contributions.

2. **Grants**

	Restricted £	Unrestricted £	Total £	Total £
Central Government Grants	203,235	–	203,235	195,760
Local Government Grants	62,853	113,766	176,619	210,465
Health Authority Grants	385,520	–	385,520	305,000
Grant Making Trusts	79,500	49,000	128,500	93,400
Grants for the Purchase of Fixed Assets	–	–	–	10,000
Other Grants	6,750	10,000	16,750	21,500
Deferred Income Brought Forward	40,000	–	40,000	15,000
Grants Received and Receivable	777,858	172,766	950,624	851,125
Less: Amounts Deferred:				
Local Government Grant 1997/98	(20,000)	–	(20,000)	(40,000)
Grants Receivable	757,858	172,766	930,624	811,125

Note 3 – Total Resources Expended

There is no set format for this note, but the example complies with the recommendation that the natural classification of expenditure should be given as well as the activity based classification in the SOFA. This format also gives a reader sufficient understanding of the component elements of each expenditure heading. A lot of the expenditure headings have been allocated across several cost centres; the basis will need to be followed consistently.

CAMBERWICK SERVICES FOR THE MENTALLY ILL
NOTES TO THE ACCOUNTS
For the year ended 31 March 1997

3. Total Resources Expended

Resources expended represent the following direct and apportioned costs:

	Residential Services £	Day Care £	Other Projects £	Support Costs £	Fundraising & Publicity £	Management Admin. £	1997 Total £	1996 Total £
Staff Costs	452,327	153,882	104,620	76,218	20,165	3,599	810,811	665,239
Agency Cover	58,301	18,553	–	–	–	–	76,854	70,964
Training and Recruitment	3,434	5,928	6,402	–	–	–	15,764	13,519
Care and Welfare	21,762	3,233	–	–	–	–	24,995	22,520
Provisions and Activities	52,463	25,874	3,195	–	–	–	81,532	78,686
Premises and Equipment	134,373	38,995	22,324	13,698	845	–	210,235	218,221
Communications	4,521	1,642	1,875	6,631	1,040	3,061	18,770	16,925
Legal and Professional	1,100	–	–	5,422	–	7,852	14,374	16,111
Depreciation	10,439	1,125	–	5,177	–	–	16,741	14,343
Other	4,046	7,073	3,371	1,326	–	–	15,816	12,717
	742,766	256,305	141,787	108,472	22,050	14,512	1,285,892	1,129,245

Note 4 – Net Incoming Resources Before Transfers

This is a requirement of the Companies Act formats. If the information is given elsewhere, then it could, in fact, be omitted. It is only necessary to disclose certain items if they apply.

Note 5 – Transfer Between Funds

Any transfers between funds must be shown gross, not netted off. The note should explain the reason for the transfer and any circumstances which are relevant e.g. the terms of a legacy.

Note 6 – Interest Payable

Companies Act format requires analysis of interest payable into separate categories as to whether the loans are repayable in the next year, the next five years or longer term.

Note 7 – Staff Costs and Numbers

The Companies Act format requires staff costs to be analysed into gross salary and employer's national insurance contribution (social security costs) and pension contributions or other benefits. The number of staff employed needs to be given as an average for the year, analysed into appropriate categories of activities.

The SORP requires the amount of total staff emoluments to be disclosed, as well as an analysis of the emoluments of higher paid employees into bands, commencing at £40,000 and going up in bands of £10,000. If a band does not apply, then it need not be shown. The number of employees remunerated within each band has to be shown. Remuneration should be the definition for tax purposes i.e. emoluments to include benefits, use of car etc.

CAMBERWICK SERVICES FOR THE MENTALLY ILL
NOTES TO THE ACCOUNTS
For the year ended 31 March 1997

4. Net Incoming Resources Before Transfers	1997	1996
This is stated after charging/crediting:	£	£
Remuneration to Auditors	4,994	4,700
Depreciation	16,741	14,343
Interest Payable (Note 5)	825	964
Hire of Equipment	10,162	9,446
Interest Receivable	2,098	4,402

5. Transfer Between Funds

The amount of £19,000 was transferred from unrestricted funds to restricted funds as a contribution to the Minor Tranx project, being general fundraising funds the directors wish to apply to this project.

6. Interest Payable

	1997	1996
	£	£
On Bank Loans, Overdrafts and Other Loans Wholly Repayable Within 5 Years	825	964

7. Staff Costs and Numbers

Charity

	1997	1996
Salaries and Wages	730,867	600,167
Social Security Costs	73,880	59,365
Other Pension Costs	6,064	5,707
	810,811	665,239

The average number of staff employed by the charity during the year was as follows (full time equivalent):

	No.	No.
Residential Services and Management	27	25
Day Care	9	7
Other Projects	6	3
Support and Administration	5	5
	47	40

The total emoluments of staff were £730,867 (1996 – £600,167) and the number of employees whose total emoluments exceeded £40,000 was as follows:

	1997	1996
£40,000 – £50,000	1	1

Note 8 – Taxation

Companies Act format requires the amount of tax payable to be shown. Since charities generally have no tax to pay, the note could be omitted, but it is included to clarify the basis and tax status of the charity and its subsidiary.

Note 9 – Tangible Fixed Assets

The different categories of fixed assets are shown in this example. Cost, depreciation and net book value should be shown as brought forward figures, change in year and carried forward figure. In this example, there are also disposals, which have to be shown separately to additions in the year.

CAMBERWICK SERVICES FOR THE MENTALLY ILL
NOTES TO THE ACCOUNTS
For the year ended 31 March 1997

8. Taxation

All of the charity's income is applied for charitable purposes and therefore the charity is exempt from corporation tax. The charity's trading subsidiary has no corporation tax liability (1996: £nil) because profits on the sale of purchased goods are transferred by gift aid to Camberwick Services for the Mentally Ill.

9. Tangible Fixed Assets

	Freehold Land & Buildings	Motor Vehicles £	Furniture & Equipment £	Total £
Group and Charity				
COST OR VALUATION				
At 1 April 1996	180,000	17,646	49,183	246,829
Additions in Year	–	18,325	7,105	25,430
Disposals in Year	–	(17,646)	–	(17,646)
At 31 March 1997	**180,000**	**18,325**	**56,288**	**254,613**
DEPRECIATION				
At 1 April 1996	–	13,235	25,920	39,155
Charge for Year	–	4,581	12,160	16,741
Eliminated on Disposal	–	(13,235)	–	(13,235)
At 31 March 1997	**–**	**4,581**	**38,080**	**42,661**
NET BOOK VALUE				
At 31 March 1997	**180,000**	**13,744**	**18,208**	**211,952**
At 31 March 1996	**180,000**	**4,411**	**23,263**	**207,674**

The freehold property was valued by A R W Martin ARICS on 18 March 1996 on an open market basis in accordance with guidelines issued by the Royal Institution of Chartered Surveyors. The property has been given as security for the loan from Wickshire County Council (Note 13)

All fixed assets were for direct charitable purposes

Note 10 – Investments

The investment for this organisation are the shares in the subsidiary. It is necessary to give the summarised results of the trading subsidiary so that the size and profitability of the subsidiary can be gauged.

Note 11 – Stock

If the charity has stock in the balance sheet, the note needs to explain the nature of the stock e.g. raw materials, finished goods.

CAMBERWICK SERVICES FOR THE MENTALLY ILL
NOTES TO THE ACCOUNTS
For the year ended 31 March 1997

10. Investments

	The Group		The Charity	
	1997	1996	1997	1996
	£	£	£	£
Investment in Subsidiary Undertaking at Cost	–	–	100	100

Net Income from Trading Activities of Subsidiary

The charity holds 100% of the issued ordinary share capital of Trading Company Limited, a company incorporated in England and Wales. Trading Company Limited sells purchased and donated goods.

Relevant financial information regarding Trading Company Limited is as follows:

	1997	1996
	£	£
Turnover	44,986	44,873
Cost of Sales	(15,272)	(13,853)
Gross Profit	29,714	31,020
Other Operating Income	96	178
Administrative Expenses	(14,558)	(13,936)
Interest Payable	(102)	(128)
Net Profit Before Taxation	15,150	17,134
Corporation Tax	–	–
Net Profit After Taxation	15,150	17,134
Transferred to Care for The Mentally Ill	(13,000)	(14,000)
Retained in Subsidiary	2,150	3,134

The results of Trading Company Limited have been consolidated on the basis of the net profit before transfers to Care for The Mentally Ill. The gross income of the group totals £1,367,218 (1996: £1,227,879) and the gross expenditure totals £1,315,824 (1996: £1,157,162).

11. Stock

	The Group		The Charity	
	1997	1996	1997	1996
	£	£	£	£
Purchased Goods for Resale	2,162	1,854	–	–

Note 12 – Debtors

Any breakdown of the debtors total shown on the balance sheet which will help a reader to understand the nature of the amounts due should be given. The minimum required is an analysis into:

◆ trade debtors

◆ amounts owed by connected bodies

◆ other debtors

◆ prepayments

This has to be given for both the charity and the group to explain both sets of figures on the balance sheet.

Note 13 – Creditors: Amounts Due Within One Year

It is a requirement to show separately in this note:

◆ loans and overdrafts

◆ trade creditors

◆ amounts due to any connected body

◆ other creditors

◆ accruals and deferred income

Headings may be omitted where there is nothing to state against them; additional headings may be included for clarification. The amounts need to be given for both the group and the charity.

Note 14 – Creditors: Amounts Falling Due After More Than One Year

The details of the creditor must be given, such as the loan terms and the scheduled repayment date.

CAMBERWICK SERVICES FOR THE MENTALLY ILL
NOTES TO THE ACCOUNTS
For the year ended 31 March 1997

12. Debtors

	The Group		The Charity	
	1997	1996	1997	1996
	£	£	£	£
Grants Receivable	23,729	25,510	23,729	25,510
Residents' Arrears	10,625	12,507	10,625	12,507
Amounts Due From Subsidiary Undertaking	–	–	5,816	4,375
Other Debtors	2,539	3,094	2,539	3,094
Prepaid Expenses	2,122	1,764	1,722	1,764
	39,015	42,875	44,431	47,250

13. Creditors: Amounts Falling Due Within One Year

	£	£	£	£
Wickshire County Council Loan (Note 13)	10,000	10,000	10,000	10,000
Residents' Charges Received in Advance	26,272	18,511	26,272	18,511
Taxation and Social Security	30,431	35,443	30,431	34,086
Pension Contributions	6,064	5,707	6,064	5,707
Other Creditors	42,715	25,046	41,457	24,946
Accruals and Deferred Income	69,732	84,810	67,232	81,842
	190,226	175,505	185,111	171,437

14. Creditors: Amounts Falling Due After One Year

	1997	1996
	£	£
Group and Charity		
Wickshire County Council Loan	10,000	20,000

The loan from the Wickshire County Council was advanced on 1 October 1990 and is repayable over four years commencing on 1 April 1994. Interest is charged at 2.75% per annum on the reducing balance after 1 April 1995. The loan is secured on the freehold property, and the total due under the loan is as follows:

	£	£
Amounts falling due within one year (Note 12)	10,000	10,000
Amounts falling due after one year	10,000	20,000
Total	20,000	30,000

Note 15 – Analysis of Net Assets Between Funds

The assets and liabilities of the charity must be identified to the particular fund. Where there has been a revaluation, it is a requirement of the Companies Acts that the amount of the reserves attributable to the revaluation should be shown.

Note 16 – Restricted Funds

The note needs to explain what the total balance carried forward in the balance sheet relates to. It is helpful to identify how the restricted fund will be used in the future.

Note 17 – Total Funds

Where group accounts have been prepared and only a consolidated SOFA is presented, a note needs to explain the movements on the funds of the subsidiary. The example here shows the movement on all funds for clarity, and ties the amounts in to the balance sheet and note 16 above.

CAMBERWICK SERVICES FOR THE MENTALLY ILL
NOTES TO THE ACCOUNTS
For the year ended 31 March 1997

15. Analysis of Group Net Assets between Funds

	Restricted Funds £	Unrestricted Funds £	Total Funds £
Fund balances at 31 March 1997 as represented by:			
Tangible Fixed Assets	5,000	206,952	211,952
Current Assets	62,457	225,286	287,743
Liabilities	(20,000)	(180,226)	(200,226)
Total Net Assets	47,457	252,012	299,469
Unrealised gains included above on Tangible Fixed Assets	–	134,835	134,835

16. Restricted Funds

	At 1 April 1996	Incoming £	Outgoing £	At 31 Mar 1997 £
Day Care Project	–	295,914	(256,305)	39,609
Minor Tranx Project	538	27,258	(25,516)	2,280
Advocacy Project	2,827	14,663	(16,922)	568
Fixed Asset Fund	7,500	–	(2,500)	5,000
Residential Services	–	389,933	(389,933)	–
Other	–	51,090	(51,090)	–
	10,865	778,858	(742,266)	47,457

Balances on restricted funds at 31 March 1997 for the Day Care, Minor Tranquillisers and the Advocacy projects are specified funds which will be applied to those projects in the coming year.

The balance on the fixed asset fund at 31 March 1997 represents the balance of grants for the purchase of fixed assets received not yet expended by depreciation on the related assets.

17. Total Funds

	At 1 April 1996 £	Incoming £	Outgoing £	Transfers £	At 31 Mar 1997 £
The movements on funds were:					
Restricted Funds	10,865	759,858	(742,266)	19,000	47,457
Unrestricted Funds:					
• Charity General	98,094	562,278	(543,626)	(6,000)	110,746
• Revaluation Fund	134,835	–	–	–	134,835
Subsidiary	4,281	45,082	(29,932)	(13,000)	6,431
	248,075	1,367,218	(1,315,824)	–	299,467

Note 18 – Commitments Under Operating Leases

If an organisation has operating leases, then it is a requirement to shown the annual commitments under those leases. An operating lease can be a photocopier lease or the lease on premises. SSAP 21 requires disclosure, with the analysis between leases according to their expiry date.

Note 19 – Trustees' Remuneration and Expenses

A note must be included even if the amounts of both remuneration and expenses were nil. There is no need to detail who received the expenses, but the total paid out and the nature of the expenses should be stated. Trustees should not be remunerated unless special consent has been given by the Charity Commission.

Note 20 – Indemnity Insurance

If the charity has paid the premiums on insurance to indemnify the trustess against claims for losses arising from negligence, then this has to be disclosed.

Note 21 – Remuneration of Auditors

The SORP requires the analysis of fees paid to auditors between fees for audit and fees for other services, with further analysis of the other services to describe them adequately.

CAMBERWICK SERVICES FOR THE MENTALLY ILL
NOTES TO THE ACCOUNTS
For the year ended 31 March 1997

18. Commitments Under Operating Leases

As at 31 March 1997, annual commitments under non-cancellable operating leases were as follows:

	1997		1996	
	Land and Buildings £	Office Equip. £	Land and Buildings £	Office Equip. £
Group and Charity				
Leases Expiring:				
Within One Year	–	1,800	–	–
Within Two to Five Years	24,650	7,095	–	8,895
After Five Years	57,200	1,040	81,850	–
	81,850	9,935	81,850	8,895

19. Trustees' Remuneration and Expenses

The directors of the charitable company are the trustees under charity law and received no remuneration, either from the charity or its trading subsidiary.

Six trustees received reimbursement for travel costs for attending meetings which amounted to £585 in total (1996 – £536).

20. Indemnity Insurance

The charity paid for the insurance premiums to indemnify directors and senior staff from any loss arising from the neglect or defaults of directors or staff and any consequent loss.

21. Remuneration to Auditors

The total paid to the auditors for the group related to the following services:

	1997 £	1996 £
Audit	3,640	3,000
Accountancy	1,354	1,700
	4,994	4,700

Chapter 8

AUDIT

A statutory audit requirement is new for unincorporated charities, as this was not part of the 1960 Charities Act. However, many charities will have had their accounts audited prior to the introduction of Part VI of the 1993 Act. It is commonly a requirement in the trust deed or constitution; trustees may also have chosen to have an audit to obtain added assurance that the financial statements did show a true and fair view, to obtain assistance from auditors in the presentation of the financial statements and other professional advice.

Many charities had an honorary audit, some had an accountant or other financially competent person review the accounts. There were all sorts of informal arrangements which will no longer be allowed. In England and Wales, unincorporated charities with gross income or total expenditure exceeding £10,000 will have to have an independent examination or an audit if their gross income or total expenditure exceeds £250,000.

A significant number of charities are incorporated, either as companies or Industrial and Provident Societies. These charities have to follow the relevant legislation i.e Companies Acts or Industrial and Provident Societies Acts. Chapter 1 sets out the requirements for audit for unincorporated charities and charitable companies in detail.

New guidelines for auditors are published to replace the 1981 Charities Auditing Guideline. The Audit Practice Note for Charities being published in 1996 by the Auditing Practices Board. It goes through the Statements of Auditing Standards (SAS) and draws out where there are particular points of importance when auditing charities. This is essential reading for every charity auditor.

Form of Accounts

Accounting standards and financial reporting standards apply to charity accounts, as they do to any undertaking where there is a requirement for the financial statements to give a true and fair view. This will not be the case where the auditor is reporting on a receipts and payments account and statement of assets and liabilities.

For the vast majority of charities, the form of accounts will need to follow the Statement of Recommended Practice for Charities (SORP). As the SORP is recommended practice, auditors should assume that following the recommendations will give a true and fair view. Departures from the SORP will mean that accounts are unlikely to give a true and fair view, but if a departure from the SORP is necessary in order for the accounts to give a true and fair view, then it can be justified. The departure would need to be explained and the effect quantified.

Unincorporated charities must comply with the accounting regulations, but since these are based on the SORP, then compliance with the regulations can be assumed if compliance with SORP has been checked. However, the SORP covers more matters than the regulations and so if there is non-compliance with the SORP on a certain matter then the regulations may have to be checked.

Charitable companies will need to comply with the Companies Act 1985 with respect to the form and content of their accounts. They may depart from the requirements of Schedule 8 and prepare a Statement of Financial Activities (SOFA) instead of a profit and loss account, on the grounds of a true and fair override and that compliance with the SORP requires it. However, charitable companies will usually need to prepare a summary income and expenditure account in addition to the SOFA in order to comply with Companies Act requirements. This may not be necessary for some charities where the SOFA can be adapted in layout to also provide all the information in an income and expenditure account.

Charitable Industrial and Provident Societies should follow the SORP. The current format of accounts for Industrial and Provident Societies is determined by the annual return, but Societies are now permitted to submit typed accounts instead of completing the detailed return. It is anticipated that the Registrar of Friendly Societies will accept the accounts of charitable Industrial and Provident Societies in the SORP format.

The charities SORP does not apply to universities and higher education colleges, who follow a more specialised SORP (the HEI SORP). Similarly, registered housing associations should follow SORP 3 and have to comply with the Housing Associations Act 1985 and the Registered Housing Associations (Accounting Requirements) Order 1992 or the Registered Housing Associations (Accounting Requirements) (Wales) Order 1994.

Auditors should also note that the accounting regulations under Part VI of the Charities Act 1993 specify a different form of accounts for common investment funds. The charities SORP will not apply to these types of charities, to which the IMRO SORP applies, as for unit trusts.

Duties of Auditors

Auditors reporting under the Companies Acts or Friendly and Industrial and Provident Societies Acts have their duties spelled out in those acts. These are unchanged by charity legislation.

The duties of auditors reporting on unincorporated charities are new and are set out in The Charities (Accounts and Reports) Regulations 1995 (the accounting regulations) under section 44 of Part VI of the Charities Act 1993.

An auditor is required to give an opinion as to whether the accounts give a true and fair view of the state of the charity's affairs and of its incoming resources and application of resources for the year (or alternatively that the receipts and payments account and statement of assets and liabilities are properly presented). In addition, an auditor must:

- state whether the accounts have been properly prepared in accordance with the regulations

- report if proper accounting records have not been kept – report if the accounts do not agree with the underlying records

- report if there is any inconsistency between the annual report and the financial statements (if accruals accounts)

- report if he has not received all the information and explanations he considered necessary

- in the case of accounts on the receipts and payments basis, state whether they adequately distinguish any material special trust or other restricted fund of the charity

All audits have to be undertaken in accordance with Statements of Auditing Standards (SAS) issued by the Auditing Practices Board (APB). The APB produces additional guidance on the application of SAS's to particular specialised sectors.

Audit Matters for Charities

The SORP introduces some new approaches to accounts and therefore some new matters requiring attention at the audit. This chapter is not a comprehensive review of the audit of charities and does not examine all important aspects of charity audits. It is merely drawing attention to a few matters which are new as a result of the SORP.

Restricted Incoming Resources

The auditor will have to verify the classification of incoming resources and expenditure into the various funds of the charity. Procedures need to be adopted to confirm that all restricted incoming resources have been recognised as such. Larger charities should have clear guidelines and procedures for identifying incoming restricted funds, to ensure that these are recorded as such. The procedures need to be reviewed and then tests undertaken to ensure that they have been followed. This may involve a review of correspondence relating to grants, donations and bequests or a review of appeal literature. Such a review would also be necessary in a smaller charity. The auditor cannot confine his audit work to the accounting records themselves in this matter. At the planning stage, it is helpful to read the trustees' annual report, if available, or have a meeting with a senior person in the charity to hear about the work of the charity in general terms over the last year. This will often provide a good starting point for understanding the type of income the charity receives.

It will sometimes be difficult to identify whether income is restricted or not. If the grant award letter or correspondence accompanying a donation specifies what the money should be used for and this is narrower than the charity's objects, then it should be treated as a restricted fund. Legally, the trustees are receiving these funds under a special trust and will have to pass the funds back to the donor if they cannot be applied in the terms set out. Permission has to be sought from the Charity Commission if the terms cannot be fulfilled and the charity wishes to transfer the funds to unrestricted funds to be spent on its general charitable objects.

Some discussion may be necessary with senior personnel of the charity where it is not clear whether the funds should be treated as restricted or not. Direct confirmation with the donor may be considered necessary where the sums are significant.

Expenditure on Restricted Funds

The expenditure has to be allocated between the funds on a reasonable and proper basis. The auditor needs to verify that the expenditure allocated to the restricted funds does comply with the terms of the funding and has been spent on the purposes for which the monies were given. This will not be difficult where there are significant direct costs of a particular project which can be clearly identified to a specific source of funding. However, there will also have to be a consideration of a fair allocation of overheads, including staff time. Auditors will have to consider the method and basis adopted for any such allocation or apportionment of staff time and office overheads. The method should be fair and should reflect the actual costs. It should be applied consistently, as otherwise this would throw doubt on whether the basis is fair. There is obviously room for manipulation of the results and this must be checked carefully.

A useful audit technique is to review the project budgets, as these will usually have been prepared with allocated and apportioned costs. Analytical review techniques will assist the auditor to identify where the final accounts appear to diverge from the expected expenditure levels.

Charities also need to be advised to ensure that they do obtain funds on a basis which will allow them to apportion some office overheads as expenditure. A charity cannot realistically expect to spend all restricted funds only on the direct costs of projects, unless it has significant sources of unrestricted income.

Expenditure Categories

Except for the smaller charities with gross income below £100,000, charities must also categorise expenditure into headings:

> Direct charitable expenditure
>
> Fundraising and Administration
>
> Management and Administration of the Charity

Within these categories, expenditure may be restricted or unrestricted. The direct charitable expenditure will be identified to grant-giving or services provided by type of activity as appropriate to the charity's circumstances. The classification of costs into these headings will invariably involve allocation and apportionment of costs, and therefore a certain amount of subjectivity.

Audit procedures will need to ensure that the cost allocations are undertaken on some reasonable basis and consistently followed.

Fund Balances

The funds carried forward will effectively have been audited by auditing the incoming resources, expenditure and any transfers and revaluations. However, it may be appropriate to obtain further evidence concerning the fund balances being carried forward, especially where it is difficult to verify the allocation of expenditure. By looking at the activity on specific restricted funds after the balance sheet date, it may be easier to confirm the reasonableness of the individual balances comprising the total restricted fund carried forward at the year end.

In addition, the charity should identify the assets and liabilities belonging to each fund. This is done either by adopting the format of a columnar balance sheet or by an explanatory note to the accounts or both. As it forms part of the accounts, this information must be audited. Usually it will be possible to verify the specific assets belonging to a specific fund. For example, a restricted fund for the purchase of fixed assets can be related to the specific assets purchased. Some assets will not be clearly in one fund or another; investments and cash may be shared between funds under an informal pooling arrangement. Liabilities will normally either be specific to individual funds for particular purposes (e.g. a mortgage or an HP agreement) or they will form part of the charity's unrestricted funds. The audit procedure is to ensure that any assets that are specifically identified as belonging to a restricted fund are complete and accurate and that for the rest, the assumptions made are reasonable in view of the terms of the trust. Clearly auditors should be aware of the possiblity of finding a breach of trust if the terms of a restricted fund have not been followed.

A going concern issue may be raised by looking at the purpose of the funds and their related assets and liabilities. If the funds represent commitments, then the charity needs to have sufficient resources to meet those commitments. Not all charities have the assets already to meet all future commitments on projects, but they may be relying on future fundraising to raise the extra resources. The auditor must use his judgement as to whether the existing assets are sufficient to meet the immediate commitments and whether the fundraising plans are realistic.

A review of the fund balances may also identify the situation where a charity has been "robbing Peter to pay Paul". In other words, the incoming resources from one project in a restricted fund have been used on another project. This may be masking the fact that some projects are running at a deficit. In this situation, the trustees are possibly in breach of the special trust represented by the restricted fund. However, it has been known for this situation to arise without the trustees' knowledge. In practice, therefore, it is a matter to be brought to the immediate attention of the trustees, in order that they may put matters right.

Under the new accounting regime, it should be more difficult for this situation to arise. However, the importance of the underlying working papers must be emphasised. Although the SORP only requires the disclosure of the major restricted funds individually and the rest in total, the accounting records underlying the final accounts must contain detailed entries about each individual restricted fund. Audit effort must be directed to the working papers on each individual fund. This does mean that the audit of charities will require considerably more detail and time than the audit of many commercial undertakings.

Transfers Between Funds

Because restricted funds are either endowments for the general purposes of the charity or funds held on special trust under law, any transfers need to be carefully checked. Potentially, they could represent a breach of trust. A transfer from restricted to unrestricted funds should be made only upon proper authority in accordance with the terms of the trust or permission from the Charity Commission. Auditors need to ask for the documentation to support the transfer.

Transfers from one particular restricted fund to another restricted fund may also cause problems. The fact that the format of the accounts allows all restricted funds to be shown together does not mean that all restricted funds may be pooled. Each fund is held on special trust and the funds should be applied for the particular purposes set out in the terms of the donation.

Transfers from unrestricted funds to restricted funds are not likely to raise any legal problems. The transfer should, however, be explained in a note to the accounts. Such a transfer may be necessary in order for the charity to fulfil the terms of the restricted fund, e.g. the "matching" of grants with the charity's own resources to fund a major project. It is a decision for the trustees, but it should be expected that they would have a clear policy on such a matter.

Transfers from unrestricted funds to designated funds do not present auditors with any particular problem. This is a matter for the trustees to decide. The purpose of the designated funds should be clear and set out in a note to the accounts. Transfers may also be made from designated funds to unrestricted funds without any problem; designated funds are merely a method by which the trustees earmark unrestricted funds.

Intangible Income and Gifts in Kind

The SORP requires gifts in kind for distribution to be included under incoming resources and the appropriate expenditure heading for the charity. Similarly, intangible income should be valued and brought into the accounts at the value at which the charity would have had to purchase the services. Fixed assets donated to the charity should be shown as an incoming resource and capitalised on the balance sheet. Such transactions will not necessarily be documented and will probably not appear in the accounting records.

The importance of certain audit procedures is reinforced when considering how the auditor may obtain sufficient evidence that the incoming resources are complete. Some examples of how audit testing may be adapted to encompass an additional audit objective:

◆ Checking the fixed asset register to the physical assets may be undertaken normally to check that all the assets exist. The direction of this test should be reversed to check for any additional assets which are not in the records. Similarly, one should review the fixed asset register to check that all additions have been paid for.

◆ The analytical review of expenditure should also consider if there are expenditure headings where there is no expense, but it would be expected. Are they obtaining free goods or services?

◆ The review of the minutes of trustee meetings can be important in that they are often the only place where a gift in kind or some intangible income is recorded.

◆ A review of a charity's leaflets and promotional literature may also provide information about sponsors and funders, who may have funded the production of the leaflet direct.

It may also be appropriate to include a paragraph in the letter of representation where the trustees confirm to the auditor that all gifts in kind and intangible income has been included in the acounts.

The auditor also has to check that the charity has a policy on intangible income and consistently applies it. It is unusual to value and include volunteer time, but the SORP does recommend that the free services of professionals should be included. It may be difficult to value the free use of premises, but this is an obvious source of intangible income. Has the charity decided on a policy and explained the facts accordingly?

Going Concern

The separation of incoming resources and expenditure into restricted and unrestricted funds is more likely to highlight a deficit on "core" funding. Charities find it increasingly difficult to raise unrestricted funds and they may find themselves in the position of having balances to carry forward on restricted funds, but with a negative balance on unrestricted funds. This is a serious problem which may have gone undetected prior to the SORP, but the new format makes the position obvious, whereas it might have been masked in an overall positive balance before.

The danger in this situation is that the trustees will be unable to continue the activities of the charity without sufficient unrestricted funds and will therefore fail to fulfil the terms of the restricted funds. The balances on the restricted funds are potentially repayable to the donor, such that the charity may find itself with a shortfall of assets to meet liabilities. An insolvent situation therefore arises, which may immediately worsen when one values the charity on a break-up basis, when assets will no doubt be worth less and liabilities will crystallise.

Thus the auditor must undertake post-balance sheet work to review whether the situation has been corrected subsequent to the year end, by additional unrestricted resources becoming available, for example. Alternatively, the situation must be discussed with the trustees to establish whether they have a plan to deal with the situation. Where there is doubt, then the auditor will need to consider whether the going concern basis is appropriate and whether any doubts are adequately disclosed in the accounts. If, after considering the evidence, the auditor agrees that the going concern basis is appropriate and that the circumstances are properly disclosed in the accounts, then the audit report should not be qualified. But it may contain a paragraph drawing attention to the inherent uncertainties in the charity's position and referring to the disclosures in the accounts.

Going concern issues of this nature might be a matter where it is appropriate for the auditor to report the matter in writing to the Charity Commission. This is explained in more detail below under "Whistleblowing".

Revaluation of Investments

The SORP recommends that all investments should be revalued at market value. The accounting regulations state that the basis of the valuation of assets should be that of the SORP. So for unincorporated charities, revaluation of investments is a statutory requirement. Auditors will need to check that charities have revalued investments and that the basis of the valuation is disclosed. If the investments are property, then the date of the valuation, the name of the valuer and his or her qualifications should be given.

Fixed assets which are held for the charity's use do not have to be revalued. So property occupied by the charity, for example, can be stated at cost. It should be depreciated in accordance with SSAP 12.

Consolidated Accounts

The normal exemptions for small companies and small groups do not apply to charities following the SORP. The SORP recommends consolidation of all subsidiaries. Note that the line by line consolidation for commercial companies is not recommended by SORP for the trading subsidiaries of charities, where the trading is non-charitable. The consolidation method should bring in the net profits on one line in the SOFA under incoming resources.

Trustee Remuneration and Expenses

It is a requirement of the accounting regulations that any payments to trustees should be disclosed in a note to the accounts. The SORP requires the note even if the amounts to be shown are nil.

Indemnity Insurance

If a charity pays for insurance premiums to cover losses in the event of negligence by trustees or charity employees, then this fact should be disclosed in a note to the accounts.

Statement of Trustees' Responsibilities

Auditing standards apply to the audits of all entities where the auditor is required to give an opinion on whether the accounts give a true and fair view. Consequently SAS 600 on the reports by auditors will apply to charities just as they would to any other organisation. The statement of directors' or trustees' responsibilities is required in the trustees' annual report (directors' report) or it will have to be incorporated in to the audit report.

Example for an unincorporated charity
Statement of Trustees' Responsibilities
Under the Charities Act 1993, the trustees are required to prepare a statement of accounts for each financial year which gives a true and fair view of the state of affairs of the charity at the end of the financial year and of the incoming resources and application of resources in the year. In preparing the statement, the trustees are required to:

- select suitable accounting policies and apply them consistently;
- make judgements and estimates that are reasonable and prudent;
- state whether applicable accounting standards and statements of recommended practice have been followed, subject to any material departures disclosed and explained in the statement of accounts.
- prepare the financial statements on the going concern basis unless it is inappropriate to presume that the charity will continue its operations

The trustees are responsible for keeping proper accounting records which disclose with reasonable accuracy at any time the financial position of the charity at that time and to enable the trustees to ensure that any statement of account prepared by them complies with the regulations under section 42(1) of the Charities Act 1993. They are also responsible for safeguarding the charity's assets and hence for taking reasonable steps for the prevention and detection of fraud and other irregularities.

Example audit report – unincorporated charity
REPORT OF THE AUDITORS
TO THE TRUSTEES OF THE LADY PENELOPE CHARITABLE TRUST
We have audited the financial statements on pages ... to ... which have been prepared on the basis of the accounting policies set out on page ...

Respective Responsibilities of Trustees and Auditors
As set out on page ... , the trustees of the charity are responsible for the preparation of financial statements. It is our responsibility to form an independent opinion, based on our audit, on the financial statements and to report our opinion to you. We have been appointed as auditors under section 43 of the Charities Act 1993 and report in accordance with regulations made under section 44 of that Act.

Basis of Opinion
We conducted our audit in accordance with Auditing Standards issued by the Auditing Practices Board. An audit includes an examination, on a test basis, of evidence relevant to the amounts and disclosures in the financial statements. It also includes an assessment of the judgements made by the trustees in their preparation of the financial statements, and of whether the accounting policies are appropriate to the charity's circumstances, consistently applied and properly disclosed.

We planned and performed our audit so as to obtain all the information and explanations which we considered necessary in order to provide us with sufficient evidence to give reasonable assurance that the statements are free from material misstatement, whether caused by fraud or other irregularity or error. In forming our opinion we also evaluated the overall adequacy of the presentation of information in the financial statements.

Opinion
In our opinion the financial statements give a true and fair view of the state of the charity's affairs as at 31 December 19.. and of its incoming resources and application of resources in the year then ended and have been properly prepared in accordance with the Charities Act 1993 and The Charities (Accounts and Reports) Regulations 1995.

Charitable Companies

The audit report for charitable companies will be almost the same as for any other company, although it may be appropriate to change the terminology to "charitable company" instead of "company" and to "trustees" instead of "directors" if this is more consistent with the rest of the financial statements. It should, however, be made clear that the company directors and charity trustees are the same body of people in a charitable company. The status should be clear from the legal and administrative details given at the front of the accounts. There is no need to refer to any charities legislation, as the audit is being undertaken under company law.

It will be necessary to change the opinion paragraph, as the new format of accounts will not produce a surplus or deficit on which the auditor gives an opinion. The report for the unincorporated charity refers to the incoming resources and application of resources, as this is what is shown in the Statement of Financial Activities. The Companies Acts require income and expenditure, so the opinion paragraph should refer to both.

The following example illustrates the wording which can be used.

Example audit report – charitable company

Report of the Auditors to the Members of the Peter Perfect Charitable Trust

We have audited the financial statements on pages ... to ... which have been prepared on the basis of the accounting policies set out on page ...

Respective Responsibilities of Directors and Auditors

As set out on page ... , the directors of the company, who are also the trustees for the purposes of charity law, are responsible for the preparation of financial statements. It is our responsibility to form an independent opinion, based on our audit, on the financial statements and to report our opinion to you.

Basis of Opinion

We conducted our audit in accordance with Auditing Standards issued by the Auditing Practices Board. An audit includes an examination, on a test basis, of evidence relevant to the amounts and disclosures in the financial statements. It also includes an assessment of the judgements made by the directors in their preparation of the financial statements, and of whether the accounting policies are appropriate to the charitable company's circumstances, consistently applied and properly disclosed.

We planned and performed our audit so as to obtain all information and explanations which we considered necessary in order to provide us with sufficient evidence to give reasonable assurance that the statements are free from material misstatement, whether caused by fraud or other irregularity or error. In forming our opinion we also evaluated the overall adequacy of the presentation of information in the financial statements.

Opinion

In our opinion the financial statements give a true and fair view of the state of the charitable compnay's affairs as at 31 December 19.. and of its incoming resources and application of resources, including income and expenditure, in the year then ended and have been properly prepared in accordance with the Companies Act 1985.

Receipts and Payments Basis

Usually, charities which choose to prepare accounts on the receipts and payments basis will also choose to have an independent examination. Occasionally, however, trustees may choose to have an audit or an audit may be required under the governing instrument. Only unincorporated charities will have the option of preparing accounts on the receipts and payments basis. Auditors reporting on accounts prepared on the receipts and payments basis will not be able to give an opinion as to whether the accounts give a true and fair view.

Under regulation 6 (e) the audit report has to state whether in the auditor's opinion:

◆ the account and statement properly present the receipts and payments of the charity for the financial year in question and its assets and liabilities as at the end of that year; and

◆ the account and statement adequately distinguish any material special trust or other restricted fund of the charity.

Regulation 6 (f) gives the auditor the opportunity to report if the charity has failed in the requirements to keep proper accounting records and other matters. The auditor only has to give a negative opinion and the reasons for it; silence on any of the matters below with be taken to mean that all was satisfactory. The auditor should report if:

◆ accounting records have not been kept in respect of the charity in accordance with section 41 of the 1993 Act

◆ the account and statement do not accord with those records

◆ he has not received all the information and explanations to which he is entitled under regulation 8. Auditors should particularly note the requirement to report specifically on the adequacy of disclosure of restricted funds. Even though the charity is not preparing a SOFA, the underlying principle of keeping the funds separate is maintained.

Example audit report – receipts and payments basis

**REPORT OF THE AUDITORS
TO THE TRUSTEES OF
THE PONTYPANDY FOUNDATION**

We have audited the receipts and payments account and statement of assets and liabilities on pages ... to ... which have been prepared on the basis of the accounting policies set out on page ...

Respective Responsibilities of Trustees and Auditors

As set out on page ... , you are responsible as the charity's trustees for the preparation of the account and statement, which have been prepared under section 42(3) of the Charities Act 1993 following the guidance for accounting for smaller charities issued by the Charity Commission. It is our responsibility to form an independent opinion, based on our audit, on the account and statement and to report our opinion to you. We have been appointed as auditors under section 43 of the Charities Act 1993 and report in accordance with regulations made under section 44 of that Act.

Basis of Opinion

We conducted our audit in accordance with Auditing Standards issued by the Auditing Practices Board. An audit includes an examination, on a test basis, of evidence relevant to the amounts and disclosures in the account and statement. It also includes an assessment of the judgements made by the trustees in their preparation of the account and statement, and of whether the accounting policies are appropriate, in the context of the applicable accounting requirements, to the charity's circumstances, consistently applied and properly disclosed.

We planned and performed our audit so as to obtain all the information and explanations which we considered necessary in order to provide us with sufficient evidence to give reasonable assurance that the statements are free from material misstatement, whether caused by fraud or other irregularity or error. In forming our opinion we also evaluated the overall adequacy of the presentation of information in the account and statement, including whether any material special trust or other restricted fund is adequately distinguished.

Opinion

In our opinion the account and statement of assets and liabilities properly present the receipts and payments of the charity for the year ended 31 December 19.. and its assets and liabilities as at that date and have been properly prepared in accordance with the provisions of the Charities Act 1993 applicable to smaller charities.

Qualifications in Audit Reports

The basis of qualifications will be very similar as that for ordinary commercial companies and SAS 600 should be followed for the type of qualification to be given.

One specific area is non-compliance with the SORP. This could give rise to an "adverse" opinion if the departure from the SORP was material and significant, such that the financial statements did not give a true and fair view. An example of the opinion paragraph illustrates the situation where an unincorporated charity has not prepared consolidated accounts when it should have done so.

Example of an adverse opinion paragraph – unincorporated charity

Adverse Opinion

As more fully explained in note ..., consolidated financial statements have not been prepared incorporating the charity's trading and fundraising subsidiaries, as the trustees consider that the activities are fundamentally dissimiliar. In our opinion, the subsidiaries meet the criteria under which Financial Reporting Standard 2 and the Statement of Recommended Practice: Accounting by Charities require the preparation of consolidated financial statements. The consolidated net assets and net incoming resources of the group had consolidated financial statements been prepared would have been £.... and £.... respectively.

In view of the effect of the failure to consolidate the charity's subsidiaries, in our opinion the financial statements do not give a true and fair view of the charity's state of affairs as at 31 December 19.. and of its incoming resources and application of resources in the year then ended and in this respect have not been properly prepared in accordance with the Charities Act 1993 and The Charities (Accounts and Reports) Regulations 1995.

Whistleblowing

The 1993 Act imposes a new statutory duty of "whistleblowing" on charity auditors. At present, these duties only apply to the auditors of unincorporated charities. It is likely that there will be new legislation applicable to charitable companies in the near future which will bring them into the same regime. Under regulation 6(5) of The Charities (Accounts and Reports) Regulations 1995:

> "The auditor shall communicate to the Commissioners, in writing, any matter of which the auditor becomes aware in his capacity as such which relates to the activities or affairs of the charity or of any institution or body corporate connected with the charity and which the auditor has reasonable cause to believe is, or is likely to be, of material significance for the exercise, in relation to the charity of the Commissioners' functions under section 8 (general power to institute inquiries) or 18 (power to act for protection of charities) of the 1993 Act."

Under section 8 of the Charities Act 1993, the Charity Commissioners have the power to institute inquiries with regard to charities or a particular charity or class of charities, either generally or for particular purposes. These powers cannot be used to institute an inquiry into an exempt charity. The Charity Commission may obtain information as they require it and may call for documents and records to be presented to them.

Section 18 of the Charities Act 1993 gives the Charity Commissioners powers to act for the protection of charity property, where in the course of an inquiry, they are satisfied that there has been misconduct or mismanagement in the administration of a charity. Or the Charity Commissioners may consider it is necessary to act for the purposes of protecting the property of a charity or to secure its proper application for the purposes of the charity. Where either of these conditions is satisfied, the powers of the Charity Commissioners include:

◆ suspension of any trustee, officer, agent or employee

◆ appointment of additional trustees

◆ removal of a trustee, officer, agent or employee

◆ freezing of property, vesting of property in the Official Custodian, restrictions on transactions or payments

◆ appointment of a receiver and manager

Where **both** conditions are satisfied, the Charity Commissioners can:

◆ remove any trustee, officer, agent or employee implicated in the misconduct or mismanagement and/or

◆ make a scheme for the administration of the charity

The matters which may cause the auditor to report direct to the Charity Commission are therefore those which might cause the Charity Commission to instigate such action. The matter should be of "material significance". This will not necessarily be the same as materiality for the purpose of audit planning. Matters concerning the conduct of trustees may not be large sums, but may indicate that they are not acting in the best interests of the beneficiaries. In general, the types of matters which may arise which would cause an auditor to report to the Charity Commissioners are:

a) significant risk of loss to the charity arising from inadequacy in the arrangements made by the trustees for the direction and management of the charity and control of its assets

b) breaches of the trustees' powers as set out in legislation or in a particular charity's constitution or the terms of trust of a major fund of the charity

c) circumstances indicating a possible abuse of charity's property

d) failure by the trustees to notify certain matters to the Charity Commission or to obtain Charity Commission permission for certain actions

a) Auditors need to be aware of indicators that the charity is not been prudently managed. Examples of such indicators would include:

◆ a lack of control by the trustee body

◆ uncertainty over who the trustees are

- ◆ decisions and actions by a dominant staff member or one trustee are ratified without proper reporting to the other trustees and consideration of their views
- ◆ delegation to sub-committees or individuals is not controlled with adequate reports or monitoring of their activities
- ◆ important matters are not considered by the trustee body
- ◆ possible insolvency

b) Breaches of the trustees' powers as set out in legislation or in the charity's constitution or terms of trust of restricted funds may cause concern. Examples include:

- ◆ Trustees not appointed in accordance with the constitution, or the number of trustees is not in compliance. This might only be a matter of material significance if the number of trustees was too low and it means that one trustee is effectively taking all decisions. Or that the opposite is occurring, with such a large body of trustees that the management is ineffective.

- ◆ Trustees are paid remuneration when the trust deed does not permit any benefit to the trustees. This might be considered of material significance depending on the amount involved, the nature of the remuneration and the its reasonableness.

- ◆ Decisions which require professional advice are taken without advice or such advice is arbitrarily overridden.

- ◆ There is a material misapplication of funds for purposes outside the charity's objects or contrary to any special trust. For example, expenditure allocated to a restricted fund is not within the terms of the restriction.

- ◆ The trustees do not adhere to the investment powers set out in the constitution or in law with consequent material risk of loss.

Auditors need to consider carefully the impact of these circumstances as entailing a requirement to report. For example, the trustees may be receiving remuneration for their services, which is specifically disallowed by the charity's trust deed. The financial statements would not be incomplete or inaccurate if this was correctly classified and the fact disclosed, so the audit can conclude that the financial statements give a true and fair view. However, this may be a matter which should be reported to the Charity Commission. It may also be necessary to state in the audit report that the trust deed has not been complied with.

A further example of a matter to be reported would be the investment of the charity's funds inappropriately, with undue risk to the charity or to the detriment of some beneficiaries. Since charity trustees are under a duty to maximise the return from assets and specifically investments, special care must be taken in this area. Trustees should consider taking specialist advice before making an investment. If they act against the advice, then they could be held to have been negligent.

Charity auditors need to be aware of the charity's own constitution and refer to it during the audit, not just at the commencement of the engagement. They also need to be aware of charity law in general and specifically those laws which impose duties on trustees.

c) Circumstances indicating a possible serious abuse of charity's property must be reported to the Charity Commission. Any evidence that substantial property may have been misappropriated or misapplied must be reported. Transactions with connected parties will be relevant in this respect, as they may cause a conflict of interest and are a possible route to a defalcation of funds.

d) Failure by the trustees to notify certain matters to the Charity Commission or to obtain Charity Commission permission for certain actions may have to be reported. Examples of such matters are:

◆ Trustees must obtain the permission of the Charity Commission before making a substantial ex-gratia payment.

◆ The transfer of restricted funds to unrestricted funds

◆ An amendment of the constitution

The "whistleblowing" duties of auditors as set out in the regulations specifically refer to matters which come to their attention in the course of their work as auditors. In practice, auditors often provide other services to their clients and may receive information in the course of providing other services. In addition, it has already been noted that these duties do not yet apply to auditors of charitable companies. The Audit Practice Note states that it is expected that in those cases auditors would need to report such matters to the Charity Commission as a matter of public interest.

Resignation

Another new provision of the regulations provides for auditors to make a written statement to trustees, if they cease to hold office for any reason. It is an requirement for the auditor to give details of any circumstances connected with his ceasing to hold office which should be brought to the attention of trustees or a statement that there are none. A copy of the statement must also be sent to the Charity Commission. The sorts of matters which might cause an auditor to report under this regulation include:

◆ disagreement over the audit opinion

◆ disagreement over any disclosure made or to be made to the Commissioners in respect of any matter of material significance

◆ disagreement over any accounting policy, assumption, financial judgement or disclosure made in the accounts or in the preparation of the accounts

◆ concerns over any matter which is believed to give rise to a material risk of a loss of charitable funds

◆ lack of co-operation or obstruction in the context of the audit

There is no set timescale, but it is normal practice for such a letter to be produced at the same time as the resignation itself.

Reports in Relation to Land Transactions

The Charities Act 1993 brings in new procedures for charities in relation to land transactions. These may be relevant for auditors, as failure to comply with the procedures might cause the auditors to report the matter to the Charity Commission.

The new procedures are generally going to mean a relaxation of the rules for many charities, in the sense that they will no longer have to go to the Charity Commission for permission to dispose of land in every case, as was the situation prior to the 1993 Act. This did not apply to exempt charities and these new provisions similarly do not apply to them. The transactions concerned relate to disposals of land or property, whether by sale of a freehold or the granting of a long lease. A long lease for the purposes of this section is one which is more than seven years. Section 36 allows charities to dispose of such property without permission from the Charity Commission or the courts if the charity complies with certain conditions:

- the trustees must obtain and consider a written report by a qualified surveyor
- the property should be advertised as the surveyor advises
- the trustees should be satisfied that the best terms should be obtained if they follow the course of action recommended by the surveyor

If the sale or disposal is to a connected party, then the above procedures will not be sufficient and the permission of the Charity Commission should be sought for the transaction.

If the disposal is a short lease, then the advice should be from a competent person, but does not have to be from an external qualified surveyor or valuer. This means that a trustee or member of staff who is suitably qualified could provide the trustees with the advice they require. The trustees are still required to consider the advice and consider whether they will obtain the best terms if they follow the advice.

If the land or property is held under specific trusts which stipulate that it should be used for particular purposes or for the purposes of the charity, then public notice should be given of the proposed disposal. The trustees should take into account any representations made to them. These additional requirements do not apply if the charity will replace the property or is the disposal is a lease of two years or less.

Charities may dispose of land to other charities or to beneficiaries under favourable terms to the purchaser.

Reports on Mortgages

In a similar way, under section 38, charity trustees have to get proper financial advice prior to mortgaging charity property. No permission needs to be sought from the Charity Commission or the courts if the procedures have been followed. Advice needs to be obtained in writing concerning the following:

- whether the loan is necessary in order for the charity trustees to pursue the particular course of action in connection with which the loan is being sought by them;

- whether the terms of the proposed loan are reasonable having regard to the status of the charity as a prospective borrower; and

- the ability of the charity to repay on those terms the sum proposed to be borrowed.

The advice should be sought from someone who is reasonably believed by the charity trustees to be qualified by ability and experience in financial matters and who has no financial interest in the making of the loan. The person may be an employee of the charity.

Charity auditors may well be asked for a written report under section 38 and clearly each individual case has to be considered on its merits. However, certain information will obviously be helpful:

- the purpose of the loan

- the terms of the loan, including interest rates, arrangement fees, repayment schedule

- how the income to repay the loan is to be generated, supported by cashflow projections

In certain cases, it is not appropriate for charities to mortgage property and the trustees would be better advised to consider other fundraising methods which do not involve a loan. A bank considering the loan application from the charity may require the written report from the independent financial adviser prior to agreeing to the loan. This will be to ensure that the trustees have followed the law in the transaction so that it will not be invalidated by a failure to follow section 38. Clearly, any such written report is confidential between the trustees and their advisor, although the trustees may disclose its contents to their banker if they wish.

Summarised Accounts

Charities sometimes wish to print summarised accounts in the annual report. The SORP introduces new recommendations for the content and presentation of such summarised accounts.

Summarised accounts should be a fair and accurate summary of the full accounts. The full report and accounts should always be produced in addition to any summary. Summarised accounts should contain information relating to both the Statement of Financial Activities and the Balance Sheet.

Summarised accounts should be accompanied by a statement, signed on behalf of the trustees, that they are a summary of information extracted from the annual accounts.

They must also contain a warning statement, alerting readers to the fact that summarised accounts may not contain sufficient information for a full understanding of the charity's affairs. (example below) It should also state when the annual accounts were appproved, whether the accounts have been submitted to the Charity Commission and Companies House (companies only).

The statement should say if whether the accounts have been audited or not, and whether the opinion of the auditor was qualified or not. If the report was qualified, then an explanation of the qualification may be necessary. It will only be appropriate to publish the full audit report if the full accounts are also published with it.

The auditor needs to give an opinion as to whether the summarised accounts are consistent with the full accounts

---

Example Statement by Trustees

These summarised accounts are a summary of information extracted from the audited annual accounts, on which the auditors' opinion was unqualified. The full report and accounts were aproved by the trustees on 13 September 1997 and have been submitted to the Charity Commission and the Registrar of Companies. These summarised accounts may not contain sufficient information to allow for a full understanding of the financial affairs of the charity. For further information the full accounts, the auditor's report on those accounts and the Trustees' Annual Report should be consulted. Copies of these may be obtained from the Secretary at The Works, Islington High Street, London, N1.

Signed on behalf of the Trustees

Jo Bloggs

20 September 1997

Example Auditors' Statement with Summarised Accounts

As auditors to the charity, we have reviewed the summarised accounts above and consider that they are consistent with the full accounts, on which we gave our opinion.

Signed – Auditors

Date

Statement of Auditing Standard

Under SAS 160, auditors are also required to review the written report being published with financial statements. Auditors need to check that there is no inconsistency between the financial statements and the narrative report. If they find any problems, then this would be brought to the attention of the management and trustees in the first instance. In the rare situation where the error is not rectified, then the auditors would have to take the further step of circulating a statement to all possible readers of the report, drawing their attention to the inconsistency. This will include the trustees' report issued with the full audited accounts, but also the glossy annual report published by some charities.

Chapter 9

INDEPENDENT EXAMINATIONS

Unincorporated charities with gross income or total expenditure below £250,000 may choose to have an independent examination instead of an audit. The concept of independent examination is a new one, introduced for the first time in the Charities Act 1993. It only applies to unincorporated charities, not companies or Industrial and Provident Societies.

Scope of Examination

The idea is to allow those with some accounting skills, but not necessarily registered auditors, to undertake a review of the accounts of smaller charities. The independent examination is not as rigorous as an audit, mainly because the independent examiner is not required to give an opinion that the financial statements "give a true and fair view". The independent examiner is expected to give "negative assurance", that is to say that he or she did not come across anything in the course of their examination which makes them doubt the reasonableness of the accounts so presented. The auditor, on the other hand, is under a positive duty to seek out evidence to support the view given by the accounts.

The independent examiner is obliged to undertake more work than the reporting accountant under the Companies Act 1985. Accountants should therefore not confuse the two reports and should not assume that they will have completed enough work if they have prepared the accounts. Whilst it will undoubtedly be common practice for independent examiners to also prepare accounts, this will not be sufficient. The "General Directions on the Carrying Out of an Independent Examination" ("General Directions") issued by the Charity Commissioners set out more specific work which must be undertaken to gain adequate assurance on the accounts. The independent examiner must document his or her work so that it can be seen how they reached their conclusions.

Duties of Independent Examiners

The Charities (Accounts and Reports) Regulations 1995 set out the duties of independent examiners. The report by an independent examiner should state whether or not any matter has come to the examiner's attention in connection with the examination which gives him reasonable cause to believe that in any material respect:

◆ accounting records have not been kept in accordance with section 41 of the Charities Act 1993

◆ the accounts do not agree to the underlying records

◆ the accounts do not comply with the regulations if they are preparing a accounts on the accruals basis

◆ attention should be drawn to any matter to enable a proper understanding of the accounts

◆ there has been any material expenditure or action which appears not to be in accordance with the trusts of the charity

◆ he has not received any information or explanations requested

◆ there is any inconsistency between the accounts and annual report (where accounts have been prepared on the accruals basis)

General Directions

The work required in an independent examination is explained in the General Directions issued by the Charity Commissioners. Their publication "Guidance and General Directions on the Carrying Out of an Independent Examination" also includes guidance on how the examiner may interpret the directions and fulfil his or her duties. The guidance has not been reproduced in full here and examiners are advised to obtain a copy of the guidance from the Charity Commission.

The General Directions set out the minimum amount of work which is necessary to undertake an examination. The General Directions are set out below in bold type, with commentary and explanatory notes to follow after each section in plain type.

(a) **obtain an understanding of the charity's constitution, organisation, accounting systems, activities and nature of assets, liabilities, incoming resources and application of resources in order to plan the examination procedures appropriate to the circumstances of the charity;**

As well as a copy of the governing instrument, it is useful to obtain a copy of the trustees' annual report at the beginning, if they have prepared one. It is also useful to obtain any leaflets or brochures which describe the organisation's work. An interview or telephone conversation with a trustee or senior employee of the organisation may draw out highlights of the year. All this is to give the examiner an idea of the complexity of the organisation, significant events to look for, an idea of the appropriateness of expenditure. The examiner also needs to have some idea of the financial controls operating in the charity, so as to assess whether the records are likely to be a reliable record of what actually happened during the year. An example checklist of the sort of questions to ask in this part of the process:

1. What are the registered charitable objects?

2. Where does the main funding come from?

3. What were the main activities during the year?

4. Does the charity have any employees?

5. Does the charity have any premises?

6. Who is responsible for authorising expenditure? Who signs cheques?

7. How is income handled?

8. Do they have any cash transactions?

9. What accounting records are kept?

Depending on the answers to these, subsidiary questions may be necessary!

(b) carry out such procedures and checks as are necessary to provide reasonable assurance that an examination is required under section 43(3) and that section 43(2) (audit) does not apply to the charity, and where accounts are prepared under section 42(3), that the charity trustees may properly elect to prepare accounts under this sub-section;

This will involve a check on the gross income and total expenditure of the charity. Obviously, if the charity has exceeded the thresholds for audit or for the preparation of accounts on the accruals basis, then the independent examiner may need to consider whether he or she should withdraw from the engagement. Since the examiner is likely to prepare the accounts, then it would appropriate for the accounts preparation to be undertaken at an early stage to check this. It must be remembered that the audit requirement continues for a further two years, even if gross income and total expenditure drop below the threshold.

(c) record the examination procedures carried out, and document matters which are important to support conclusions reached or statements provided in the Examiner's report;

The independent examiner will need to write down his or her approach to the examination and document questions asked and answers received. Firms of accountants often use checklists and work programmes to assist in documenting their work. It is important that sufficient evidence of the work done is on a file to show how the conclusions in the report have been reached. An independent examiner may need to demonstrate that he or she did undertake their work carefully and responsibly. For example, they should date all working papers, so that if an event happens after the date of their examination, it can be shown that they could not have known about it.

Since the examiner is likely to be also preparing the accounts, it is usual to show some of the evidence of the examination on accounting papers. So a schedule of creditors just needs a few notes to explain which ones have been checked and the conclusion.

(d) compare the accounts of the charity with the charity's accounting records in sufficient detail to provide a reasonable assurance that the accounts are in accordance with such accounting records;

This is a basic procedure to confirm that the accounts have been properly prepared. Since the examiner will often be preparing the accounts, then this procedure will not necessarily involve a great deal of extra work. If someone else has prepared the accounts, then it will be necessary to trace figures on the draft accounts back to the trial balance and books of prime entry, such as cash books.

(e) **inspect all accounting records, in order to provide a reasonable assurance that any material or gross failures to maintain the records have been identified;**

The independent examiner has to report if proper accounting records have not been kept. Section 41 of the Charties Act 1993 requires:

(1) The charity trustees of a charity shall ensure that accounting records are kept in respect of the charity which are sufficient to show and explain all the charity's transactions, and which are such as to:

  (a) disclose at any time, with reasonable accuracy, the financial position of the charity at that time, and

  (b) enable the trustees to ensure that, where any statements of accounts are prepared by them under section 42(1) below, those statements of accounts comply with the requirements of regulations under that provision.

(2) The accounting records shall in particular contain:

  (a) entries showing from day to day all sums of money received and expended by the charity, and the matters in respect of which the receipt and expenditure takes place; and

  (b) a record of the assets and liabilities of the charity.

The normal standards of "proper accounting records" apply, so it is sufficient if the records are simple cash books, bank statements and supporting documentation. If a little work has to be done on the records to really bring them up to the standard required, then this is not a gross failure. For example, the trustees may not have ensured that a bank reconciliation was prepared, but the examiner can prepare one on behalf of the trustees. The accounting records should contain dates, so that it is possible to construct the financial picture at any date. It is not necessary for the books to be completely up to date at any given time. It is obviously good practice for books to be up to date, and an examiner would gain some reassurance that the charity was operating proper financial controls if there were regular reports, bank reconciliations etc. However, it would only be necessary to report on a failure to maintain proper accounting records if there was no way of even reconstructing the records i.e. no or few invoices, little supporting documentation for income, no records of receipts and payments.

The record of assets and liabilities does not have to be sales and purchase ledgers, which would not be appropriate to most charities. It probably does mean that the charity ought to have a fixed asset register, which can be a simple list of items with the date purchased. Liabilities may often be recorded just as a loose leaf file containing unpaid invoices.

(f) **carry out analysis and review procedures on the accounts to identify unusual items, disclosures or omissions. Where concerns arise from** these procedures, the Examiner shall seek explanations and information to explain such items, disclosures or omission from the charity trustees. If, after following such procedures, the Examiner has reason to believe that in any respect the accounts may be materially misstated then additional procedures, including verification of the asset or liability or vouching of the item of incoming resource or application, must be carried out;

It is expected that the analytical review procedures available in most cases will be sufficient for examinations. Analytical review consists of the following steps:

(1) establish what you would expect to find – this might be by reference to past year's figures, current year's budgets, narrative reports, other similar charities. Knowledge of the charity's activities is essential to this first step.

(2) undertake a comparison between expected figures and actual figures

(3) identify differences and variances which may be significant

(4) enquire into reasons for the variances

(5) obtain evidence to support the reasons given for the variances

---

Example

The charity's budget stated that they expected to receive a grant from the local authority of £60,000. In fact, the amount shown in the accounts is £58,000. The treasurer says that the final amount paid was less. The examiner should ask for the grant award letters or remittance advices from the local authority and should check these to the cash book and bank statements.

Note that where accounts are prepared on the receipts and payments basis there will be less scope for analytical review procedures, since the figures may not be comparable.

(g) **carry out such procedures as are necessary to provide a reasonable assurance that accounts prepared under section 42(1) conform to regulations as to the form and contents of accounts;**

Section 42(1) refers to full accruals accounts which will comply with the accounting regulations and will therefore include a Statement of Financial Activities and a Balance Sheet. This section does not apply to accounts prepared on the receipts and payments basis, as there is no prescribed form for the accounts. The examiner will need to check that the accounts do identify incoming resources and expenditure, assets and liabilities into capital, restricted and unrestricted funds. Unless the charity has gross income of less than £100,000, the expenditure must be categorised into direct charitable expenditure, fundraising and publicity and management and administration. Various notes to the accounts will be required and the checklist in Appendix I can be used for reference.

(h) **when accounts are prepared under section 42(1), review the accounting policies adopted and consider their conformity with** fundamental accounting concepts, consistency of application and their appropriateness to the activities of the charity. The Examiner shall also consider and review the appropriateness of any material assumptions or financial judgements that have been made in preparing the accounts;

In order to draw up accruals accounts, accounting policies need to be adopted and should be stated in the notes to the accounts. The examiner should ensure that the poicies are implemented and are appropriate. Similarly, certain assumptions and judgements are made and the examiner needs to check that these are reasonable. For example, a small housing project may have some debtors at the year end. A judgement has to be made about whether these are collectible or not and the examiner should ensure that the bad debt provision is adequate.

(i) when accounts are prepared under section 42(1), inquire of the charity trustees as to material events subsequent to the year end of the accounts examined which may require adjustment or disclosure in the accounts;

Post balance sheet events may well affect the values for certain items in the balance sheet. This will only apply to charities preparing accounts under the accruals basis. Certain events will be "adjusting events", for example receipt of an amount after the balance sheet date which refers to the period for which the accounts are being drawn up. This amount should be shown as accrued income in the accounts. A review of the accounting records and other documentation after the financial year end up to the date of the examination is necessary and the examiner should ensure that he does not limit his review to the records for the financial year only.

(j) when accounts are prepared under section 42(1), compare the accounts to any financial references in the trustees' annual report (if any): identify any major inconsistency and consider the significance such matters will have on a proper and accurate understanding of the charity's accounts;

When accounts are prepared under the accruals basis, the examiner should also read the trustees' annual report. It should be checked for inconsistencies. Normally, it will be sufficient to draw any inconsistency to the attention of the trustees. If this does not lead to an amendment in the report, then it may be necessary to refer to the matter in the examiner's report.

(k) review and assess all conclusions drawn from the evidence obtained from the examination and consider the implication on the report provided. If the Examiner has cause to make a negative statement on any matter arising from the provisions of Regulation 7(e), or to make a statement on any matter arising from the provisions of Regulation 7(f), then the Examiner shall ensure that the report provided gives a clear explanation of the matter and of its financial effects on the accounts presented together with details of any adjustments or disclosures which the Examiner believes necessary to provide the charity trustees with a proper understanding of the accounts and to ensure compliance with any relevant regulations;

Examinations of all accounts will require an overall review of the work undertaken and evidence available. The examiner should come to conclusions and document them. The examiner needs to show that he has thought about each aspect of the report and consider whether he has anything to report.

(l) **inform the Charity Commissioners in writing if, in the course of an examination or whilst acting in the capacity of the Examiner of a charity, information or evidence is obtained which gives the Examiner reasonable cause to believe such information or evidence to be relevant to the discharge of the Commissioners' functions under section 8 (general power to institute inquiries) or 18 (power to act for protection of charities).**

This gives the independent examiner "whistleblowing" duties, similar to those of charity auditors. (See Chapter 8 for a more extensive review of the matters which may arise.) The guidance produced by the Charity Commission makes it clear that it is only necessary to report where the trustees have been responsible for "deliberate or reckless misconduct". It is likely that a duty to report only arises where there is a significant loss of funds or a misapplication of funds caused by the misconduct. However, in the situation of a payment to a trustee, for example, it might be considered that any amount is significant.

Example Independent Examiner's Report

INDEPENDENT EXAMINER'S REPORT TO THE TRUSTEES OF THE LADY PENELOPE CHARITABLE TRUST

I have examined the [accounts] [account and statement] on pages ... to ... which have been prepared on the basis of the accounting policies set out on page...

Respective Responsibilities of Trustees and Examiner

The trustees of the charity are responsible for the preparation of accounts; they consider that the audit requirement under section 43(2) of the Charities Act 1993 does not apply. I have been appointed under section 43 of the Charities Act 1993 and report in accordance with regulations made under section 44 of that Act. It is my responsibility to examine the accounts, without performing an audit, and to report to the trustees.

Basis of Examiner's Statement

This report is in respect of an examination carried out under section 43 of the Charities Act 1993 and in accordance with the directions given by the Charity Commissioners under section 43(7)(b). An examination includes a review of the accounting records kept by the charity trustees and a comparison of the accounts presented with those records. It also includes a review of the accounts and making such enquiries as are necessary for the purposes of this report. The procedures undertaken do not constitute an audit.

➤ CONTINUED

> ➤ *CONTINUED*

Examiner's Statement

Based on my examination, no matter has come to my attention which gives me reasonable cause to believe that in any material respect accounting records have not been kept in accordance with section 41 of the Charities Act 1993, or that the accounts presented do not accord with those records or comply with the accounting requirements of the Charities Act 1993. No matter has come to my attention in connection with my examination to which, in my opinion, attention should be drawn to enable a proper understanding of the accounts.

J.Wright
200 Lincoln Road   Chartered Accountant
Brighton
BN2 0NQ   30 June 1997

Selection of Independent Examiners

The Charities Act 1993 specifically introduces the term "independent examiner" to describe someone who may not be a qualified accountant. Audits have to be undertaken by registered auditors, who have to work to a specified standard and undertake a minimum of work to be able to provide an audit opinion on even the smallest undertaking. The independent examiner is outside this regulated world, but has to be

> "an independent person who is reasonably believed by the trustees to have the requisite ability and practical experience to carry out a competent examination of the accounts." (Charities Act 1993, section 43(3)(a)

The Charity Commission guidance notes on independent examinations include in an appendix guidance on the selection of an examiner. The guidance strongly recommends that a qualified accountant is appointed to undertake the examination of accounts prepared under SORP and on the accruals basis (charities with gross income or total expenditure of more than £100,000). This also applies to charities with substantial assets (gross assets in excess of £1 million). Smaller charities with simple accounts may be able to find someone who is competent with accounts, although not a qualified accountant.

The onus is on the trustees to choose a suitable person as independent examiner. The Charity Commission guidance emphasises the need for the trustees to obtain suitable evidence of the prospective examiner's ability and practical experience. This would include taking up references and ensuring that the person is familiar with charity accounting and the Charities Act 1993 regulations.

Only someone outside the charity may undertake the examination, so trustees or their relatives, partners, employees are excluded, as are funders, donors and beneficiaries.

It should be noted that the appointment refers to the individual, not the firm if the individual is a partner in a firm of accountants. The report will be signed in the individual's name, although the firm's name may be added.

The trustees should agree the scope of the work the examiner will undertake in writing, as well as the terms of the appointment. This is the engagement letter, an example of which is shown below. The trustees may not limit the statutory duties of the examiner, nor restrict access to information. The trustees should be prepared to pay a reasonable fee if the examiner charges.

Example Engagement Letter

[Name of Chairman/woman of the Trustees
Name of Charity
Address ....]   [Date]

Dear [Name]

Independent Examination

The purpose of this letter is to set out the basis on which I act as independent examiner of the charity and the our respective areas of responsibility.

1. Responsibilities of trustees and examiner

1.1 As trustees of the charity, you are responsible for keeping accounting records in compliance with section 41 of the Charities Act 1993. You are also responsible for preparing accounts for each financial year which comply with the Act and the regulations made under the Act.

1.2 You are also responsible for making available to me any books, documents and other records, including minutes of trustees' meetings, and providing information and explanations as required for the purposes of my examination.

1.3 You are responsible for determining whether the charity meets the requirements for exemption from audit. I will inform you immediately if it becomes apparent that the charity requires an audit and withdraw from this engagement as examiner.

1.4 I am required under The Charities (Accounts and Reports) Regulations 1995 to consider the following matters and to report to you if:

   a) accounting records have not been kept in accordance with section 41 of the Charities Act 1993

   b) the accounts do not agree to the underlying accounting records

   c) the accounts do not comply with the regulations as to form and content

   d) any matter should be brought to the attention of a user of the accounts to enable a proper understanding of those accounts

   e) there has been material expenditure which appears not to be in accordance with the charity's trusts

   f) I have not received all the information and explanations I requested for the purpose of my examination

   g) there is an inconsistency betwen information in the annual report and the accounts, where these have been prepared on the accruals basis

➤ *CONTINUED*

➤ *CONTINUED*

2. Scope of examination

2.1 My examination will be conducted in accordance with directions issued by the Charity Commissioners for England and Wales. An examination includes a review of the accounting records and a comparison of the accounts presented with those records. It also includes a review of the accounts and making such enquiries as are necessary for the purposes of my report. The procedures undertaken do not constitute an audit.

2.2 The responsibility for the prevention and detection of fraud, error or non-compliance with law or regulations rests with yourselves.

3. Other Services

3.1 I will assist you with the preparation of accounts in the appropriate format from the accounting records. Draft accounts will be presented to you and should be carefully scrutinised prior to their finalisation. The responsibility for the preparation of the accounts rests with yourselves and I am undertaking this part of the assignment on your behalf.

4. Fees

4.1 My fees will be based on the actual amount of time spent on your affairs. Fees will be charged separately for each type of work and billed at the completion of each stage. Fees are due to be paid within 14 days of presentation.

5. Agreement of Terms

5.1 Once agreed this letter will remain effective from one year to the next, until it is replaced. We would be grateful if the terms of this engagement could be considered at a trustees' meeting. Please indicate your agreement with the terms by signing the copy letter and returning it to me.

We agree to the contents of this letter:

Signed .... Date ....
(Chairman/woman of the Trustees)

Liability and Professional Indemnity

Examiners are potentially personally liable if others rely on their report and then suffer a loss as a consequence. The limit of that liability will be determined by the scope of the independent examination. In other words, third parties cannot expect to gain the same degree of assurance from an independent examination of the accounts as they would from a full audit.

Examiners are under a duty of care and must act reasonably and responsibly. The examiner's working papers will be important evidence that he or she did act reasonably and responsibly. For example, if the papers show that information came to them showing that the trustees spent a substantial amount of restricted income funds on a project which did not meet the terms of the donation, and no reference is made to the matter in the examiner's report, then the examiner might be held to have failed in his duty to report the matter.

The level of the duty of care will depend on the examiner's ability and experience. So a higher standard of care is expected from a qualified accountant, whereas someone who no professional qualifications would not be expected to come up to the same standards.

Examiners may wish to consider professional indemnity insurance cover, so that they would be covered in the event of a claim against them. Firms of accountants will already have such cover, but it is available for individuals through good insurance brokers.

EXAMINER'S WORK PROGRAMME

	Ref	Initials	Date

1. Planning

1.1 Check signed engagement letter received back from charity

1.2 Obtain copy of governing instrument

1.3 Brief description of charity structure, details of trustees, activities and funding

1.4 Discuss any significant events or changes in the activities or personnel with a trustee or senior employee

1.5 Obtain trustees' annual report if possible

1.6 Review overall financial systems and accounting records kept

2. Confirm Threshold Criteria

2.1 Check that gross income and total expenditure for current year seem to be below £250,000 by review of draft accounts (if available) or cash book

2.2 Check that the threshold is not exceeded in either of the previous two years

2.3 Check whether gross income is less than £100,000 – do the trustees want to prepare accounts under the accruals basis or receipts and payments basis?

3. Consider and Document Approach

3.1 Has the charity drafted accounts or is this an additional service required?

3.2 Do the activities or funding suggest any special procedures are required?

Ref	Initials	Date

3.3 Are the books well kept, tidy and complete up to the date of the examination?

4. Checking Accounts to Records

4.1 Has charity prepared accounts? If so, then:

4.2 Check that draft accounts add up

4.3 Trace amounts in the accounts back to supporting schedules and extended trial balance

4.4 Check that extended trial balance adds up

4.5 Check extraction of trial balance from nominal ledger

4.5 Check nominal ledger accounts add up

4.6 Trace entries from cash books or other books of prime entry into nominal ledger

4.7 Check that cash books and other books of prime entry add up

[Adapt tests and checks where a computerised system used; note where tests do not apply e.g. where no nominal ledger]

5. Analytical Review

5.1 Obtain or prepare draft accounts

5.2 Obtain relevant comparative information such as budget for the year, previous year's figures

5.3 Perform a comparison and calculate variances

5.4 Highlight significant variances and make enquiries of trustees or responsible official

5.5 Document answers received

5.6 Check the reasons given for variances to other evidence or information and document

5.7 Assess whether the variances seem justified and supported by other evidence and write down your assessment

Sections 6 to 9 apply to accounts prepared under the accruals basis only

	Ref	Initials	Date

6. Form and Contents

6.1 Check that the SOFA and Balance Sheet comply with the regulations

6.2 Check disclosures in the notes to the accounts are complete by reference to the checklist

7. Accounting Policies

7.1 Review accounting policies and ensure that these are appropriate to the charity's circumstances

7.2 Check that all relevant accounting policies are disclosed in the notes to the accounts

7.3 Check that the accounts have been prepared in accordance with the accounting policies and that these are consistently applied

7.4 Consider any other assumptions or judgements which have been made; check that they are appropriate

8. Post Balance Sheet Events

8.1 Review the accounting records subsequent to the year end

8.2 Record any significant receipts and payments and check whether they relate to the year under review

8.3 Check that the accounts treatment of any such receipts and payments is correct

8.4 Enquire of the trustees or other responsible official whether there are any events which may require adjustment or disclosure

9. Annual Report

9.1 Read the trustees' annual report

9.2 Check that any financial references are consistent with the accounts

9.3 Discuss any inconsistency with the trustees; if they amend the annual report then no further action is required

	Ref	Initials	Date

9.4 Otherwise consider whether this is a matter which needs to be brought to the reader's attention in your report

10. Conclusions

10.1 Have proper accounting records been kept?

10.2 Do the accounts agree to the underlying records?

10.3 Do the accounts comply with the Charities Act 1993 and accounting regulations? Accruals accounts need to comply with regulations for form and content.

10.4 Is there any matter to which attention should be drawn to enable a proper understanding of the accounts?

10.5 Is there any material expenditure or action which appears not to be in accordance with the trusts of the charity?

10.6 Is the trustees' annual report consistent with the accounts?

Chapter 10

SCOTLAND AND NORTHERN IRELAND

The Charities Act 1993 only applies to charities in England and Wales; Scotland has its own legislation specifying the form of charity accounts and in Northern Ireland legislation specific to charity accounts is proposed but not yet passed at the time of writing. The Statement of Recommended Practice does, however, apply to all charities, unless they are covered by a more specific SORP as is the case for housing asociations and universities.

Incorporated charities in Scotland and Northern Ireland do follow the same accounts format and principles as charitable companies in England and Wales, although Northern Ireland has its own legislation. These charities will, however, need to amend their accounts to conform to the SORP requirements. They will be able to follow the examples given in earlier chapters of this book.

SCOTLAND

For unincorporated charities in Scotland the relevant legislation is Part I of the Law Reform (Miscellaneous Provisions) (Scotland) Act 1990 which came into force on 27 July 1992 and sets out the requirements for audit. The act requires charities to maintain accounting records and produce annual accounts. It also defines a Scottish charity as one which has been recognised by the Inland Revenue as charitable and is based in Scotland. (A charity registered with the Charity Commissioners in England and Wales could move its seat of management and control to Scotland and would then become a Scottish charity.)

Detailed requirements on the form and content of the accounts is set out in The Charities Accounts (Scotland) Regulations 1992, which became effective on 30 September 1992. Since the publication of the SORP, these regulations are under review and changes could be introduced later in 1996.

Audit Requirements

For charitable companies, this is the same for charities in Scotland as in England and Wales.

For unincorporated charities in Scotland, an audit is required if the gross income or gross expenditure exceeds £100,000 in the financial year or in either of the preceding two years. An audit is also required if the founding deed requires it.

If an audit is not required, then the charity must have an independent examination. There is no threshold for very small charities not requiring any external examination.

Annual Accounts

Scottish charities with gross receipts in excess of £25,000 must prepare accounts on the accruals basis. Below the threshold, they may choose to prepare accounts on the receipts and payments basis. This includes a statement of balances as well as a receipts and payments account. Format 2 below demonstrates this presentation.

For the larger charities, the accounts must take the form of an income and expenditure account and a balance sheet, with notes to the accounts. To comply with the SORP, a charity will need to prepare a Statement of Financial Activities (SOFA) as well as an income and expenditure account. This should be included by way of a note to the accounts in a prominent form.

An annual report by the trustees is also required and should be attached to the accounts, as should the auditor's report or examiner's statement.

Requirements of the Regulations

The Charities Accounts (Scotland) Regulations 1992 set out the minimum information needed in Schedules 1 and 2 to those regulations. Format 1 refers to accounts prepared on the accruals basis; Format 2 refers to accounts prepared on the receipts and payments basis. It is worth noting here that neither format requires the split into restricted and unrestricted funds. Restricted income funds are not referred to in the regulations, only permanent endowment funds, which do have to be accounted for separately.

Format 1

An example format for the income and expenditure account to show the headings specifically required follows. A heading may be omitted if there are no entries for the current or previous year. Comparative figures for the preceding year should be shown.

There is an overall requirement for the income and expenditure account that it should be in sufficient detail as may reasonably enable the user to gain a proper appreciation of the transactions and the surplus or deficit for the year.

The income and expenditure account should be in a columnar format, distinguishing restricted and unrestricted funds. Capital funds should not be brought into the income and expenditure account and receipts into a permanent endowment fund should not be included in the income and expenditure account.

Unrealised gains on the revaluation of investments or property should not be included in the income and expenditure account.

There is a specific requirement that the income and expenditure account should show the surplus or deficit for the year.

Transfers ("appropriations" in the Scottish terminology) should be shown on the face of the income and expenditure account and explained further in the notes to the accounts where necessary.

The remuneration of the auditor or examiner should be split between fees for their work as auditor or examiner and fees for other services; this can be on the face of the income and expenditure account or in a note to the accounts.

THE HIGHLANDS CHARITABLE TRUST
INCOME AND EXPENDITURE ACCOUNT
For the year ended 31 March 1997

	1997 £	1996 £
Income		
Realised gains on investments	X	X
Realised gains on the disposal of fixed assets	X	X
Income from investments other than land and buildings	X	X
Rents fom land and buildings	X	X
Gross income from fund raising activities	X	X
Legacies	X	X
Grants received and receivable	X	X
Donations received and receivable	X	X
Gross income from trading activities	X	X
Other income	X	X
Total Income	X	X
Expenditure		
Realised losses on investments	X	X
Realised losses on the disposal of fixed assets	X	X
Expenses of fund raising activities	X	X
Publicity expenses	X	X
Administrative costs	X	X
Remuneration of auditor or examiner	X	X
Relating directly to charitable activities:	X	X
Grants and donations made	X	X
Other expenditure	X	X
Gross expenditure on trading activities	X	X
Other expenditure	X	X
Total Expenditure	X	X
Surplus/Deficit for the Year	X	X

Balance Sheet

No example balance sheet is given as this will be in a similar format to the balance sheet for any other charity or company.

The balance sheet should indicate, wherever possible, which assets and liabilities form part of endowment and other restricted funds. This could be achieved by a note to the accounts, additional narrative on the face of the balance sheet or by adopting a columnar format for the balance sheet. Designated funds should be shown as part of the unrestricted funds of the charity.

Comparative figures for the previous year do have to be shown.

The balance sheet must be approved by the trustees and signed and dated by one trustee on their behalf. In practice, this means that the accounts should be approved at a quorate meeting of the trustees. The normal rules of the trust for voting should be followed e.g. a majority of those present can approve the accounts. Any accounts circulated must show the name of the trustee and the date on which the accounts were approved.

Notes to the Accounts

The regulations require the following to be shown as notes to the accounts. The note is only required where there is something to report in the current or preceding year. This is only a minimum and additional notes should be added if they provide helpful further explanation.

(a) accounting policies

(b) nature and purpose of each of the major funds

(c) details of the movements on permanent endowment funds

(d) unless shown elsewhere, a reconciliation of the movement on each major fund, showing the opening balance, income, expenditure, closing balance and any transfers between funds

(e) for grants to institutions, the details of grants paid where these are more than £1,000 or 2% of the gross income. If grants are to indiviuals, then separate disclosure is not required, but the total value of grants made and the number and range of grants shown.

(f) particulars of all commitments, identifying separately those in respect of specific charitable purposes

(g) contingent liabilities, including guarantees and the details of the conditions under which they may become payable

(h) any loans or liabilities secured on the assets

(i) trustee remuneration or reimbursement of expenses, if any, in aggregate. This includes any payment to a third party for making the services of a trustee available

(j) the total emoluments paid to employees and the avarage number of employees during the financial year

(k) such other information as may reasonably assist the user to understand the statement of accounts

(l) a cash flow statement where two out of the three conditions are satisfied:

◆ gross income exceeds £2 million

◆ more than 50 employees

◆ balance sheet total more than £975,000

Format 2

This is for charities choosing to prepare a receipts and payments account and statement of balances. There is an overall requirement that the account should set out the aggregate receipts and payments for the financial year in sufficient detail as may reasonably enable the user to gain a proper appreciation of the transactions and the excess of receipts over payments or payments over receipts for that year. The regulations specify the headings which should appear in the account if there is an entry for the current or preceding year.

The statement of balances has to show the movement on cash and investment assets as well as the balance at the year end, such that it can be reconciled to the receipts and payments account.

The category of "other assets" should include gifts in kind. Other assets and liabilities just have to be listed.

Investments and other assets should be identified to the funds of the charity.

THE LOWLANDS CHARITABLE TRUST
RECEIPTS AND PAYMENTS ACCOUNT
For the year ended 31 March 1997

	1997 £	1996 £
Receipts		
Proceeds of sale of investments	x	x
Proceeds of sale of fixed assets	x	x
Income from investments other than land and buildings	x	x
Rents fom land and buildings	x	x
Proceeds from fund raising activities	x	x
Legacies	x	x
Grants received	x	x
Donations received	x	x
Gross trading receipts	x	x
Other receipts	x	x
Total Receipts	**x**	**x**
Payments		
Purchases of investments	x	x
Purchases of other assets	x	x
Expenses of fund raising activities	x	x
Publicity expenses	x	x
Administrative costs	x	x
Gross trading payments	x	x
Remuneration of auditor or examiner	x	x
Relating directly to charitable activities:	x	x
Grants and donations	x	x
Other payments	x	x
Other payments	x	x
Total Payments	**x**	**x**
Excess of Receipts over Payments/ (Payments over Receipts)	**x**	**x**

THE LOWLANDS CHARITABLE TRUST
STATEMENT OF BALANCES
As at 31 March 1997

Cash and Bank Balances

Balances at 1 April 1996	X	X
Excess of Receipts over Payments/ (Payments over Receipts)	X	X
Balances at 31 March 1997	X	X

Investments

Balance at 1 April 1996	X	X
Purchased in Year	X	X
Sold in Year	(X)	(X)
Balance at 31 March 1997	X	X

Other Assets

Computer equipment purchased 1996 at a cost of £x

Liabilities

Independent examination fees for the current year £x

Telephone bill £x

Computer maintenance £x

There were no contingent liabilities

Approved by the trustees on

.... (date)

and signed on their behalf by

.... (Trustee)

Notes to the Accounts

Accounts prepared under the receipts and payments basis, the regulations specifiy that the following notes are required:

(a) the nature and purpose of each of the major funds

(b) unless shown elsewhere, a reconciliation of the movement on each major fund, showing the opening balance, receipts, payments, closing balance and any transfers between funds

(c) for grants to institutions, the details of grants paid where these are more than 2% of the gross receipts. If grants are to individuals, then separate disclosure is not required, but the total value of grants made and the number and range of grants shown.

(d) trustee remuneration or reimbursement of expenses, if any, in aggregate. This includes any payment to a third party for making the services of a trustee available

(e) such other information as may reasonably assist the user to understand the statement of accounts

Annual Report

In the regulations, this is referred to as "the report", but the requirements are similar to those under the SORP.

The requirements for the content of the report are the same for all charities, whether they are preparing accounts under the accruals basis or receipts and payments basis.

The report must be approved by the trustees and signed by one of them on behalf of the body of trustees as they authorise. Every copy of the report which is published and circulated in any form shall bear the name of the trustee who signed it.

The regulations specifically require the following to be included in the report, where applicable:

(a) Details of the legal and administrative arrangements including the nature of the founding document, the names and designations of those who are or have been, at any time during the financial year, trustees, and the manner of their appointment, the principal address of the body and details of any restrictions in the way the body may operate;

(b) an explanation of the objectives and organisational structure of the body;

(c) a review of the financial position and an explanation of the salient features of the statement of accounts;

(d) a review of the development, activities and achievements during the year;

(e) any other information necessary, for a proper appreciation of the financial position taking into account future plans and commitments;

(f) particulars of any connected body including the address and nature of the relationship; and

(g) particulars of any material transactions between connected bodies.

"Body" means the charity and refers to the term "recognised body", meaning recognised by the Inland Revenue as charitable and is the term used throughout the legislation to describe Scottish charities.

Audit Appointments

An auditor is appointed for a financial year and only removed if he becomes ineligible or incompetent. In the event of a removal, the auditor may submit a statement to the trustees setting out his observations on the circumstances of his removal. This statement shall be included in the trustees' annual report issued with the accounts.

Normally the trustees will appoint or remove the auditor, but any provisions in the founding document specifying other arrangements would take precedence.

An auditor resigning from office must submit his resignation in writing to the trustees and it will be effective from the date it is submitted or a later date if specified in the letter. The auditor shall explain any circumstances connected with his resignation in the notice of resignation. The circumstances should be explained in the trustees' annual report, or a statement there were no such circumstances included in the report.

An auditor has the right of access at all times to the records of the charity and shall be entitled to require such information and explanations from the present or former trustees as he thinks necessary for the performance of his duties.

Duties of Auditors

The auditors have to report their opinion on whether the balance sheet and the income and expenditure account have been properly prepared and whether a true and fair view is given of the state of affairs at the end of the financial year and of the surplus or deficit for the financial year. The auditor must also consider whether the information in the trustees' annual report is consistent with the accounts. If not, then the auditor must report on any inconsistencies in the audit report. The auditor must report if the charity has not kept proper accounting records, the accounts are not in agreement with the underlying records and if the auditor has not received all the information and explanations he required. The report must also state whether the auditor considers that the accounts comply with the relevant statutory requirements and the founding document.

Example Audit Report for an unincorporated Scottish charity

REPORT OF THE AUDITORS
TO THE TRUSTEES OF
THE HIGHLANDS PROTECTION TRUST

We have audited the financial statements on pages ... to ... which have been prepared on the basis of the accounting policies set out on page...

Respective Responsibilities of Trustees and Auditors

As set out on page ... , the trustees of the charity are responsible for the preparation of financial statements. It is our responsibility to form an independent opinion, based on our audit, on the financial statements and to report our opinion to you.

Basis of Opinion

We conducted our audit in accordance with Auditing Standards issued by the Auditing Practices Board. An audit includes an examination, on a test basis, of evidence relevant to the amounts and disclosures in the financial statements. It also includes an assessment of the judgements made by the trustees in their preparation of the financial statements, and of whether the accounting policies are appropriate to the charity's circumstances, consistently applied and properly disclosed.

➤ *CONTINUED*

> ➤ *CONTINUED*

We planned and performed our audit so as to obtain all the information and explanations which we considered necessary in order to provide us with sufficient evidence to give reasonable assurance that the statements are free from material misstatement, whether caused by fraud or other irregularity or error. In forming our opinion we also evaluated the overall adequacy of the presentation of information in the financial statements.

Opinion

In our opinion the financial statements give a true and fair view of the state of the charity's affairs as at 31 December 19... and of its incoming resources and application of resources including income and expenditure for the year then ended and have been properly prepared in accordance with the Law Reform (Miscellaneous Provisions) (Scotland) Act 1990, the Charities Accounts (Scotland) Regulations 1992 and the constitution of the charity.

Independent Examination

The regulations allow charities with gross income consistently below £100,000 to have an independent examination instead of an audit. Charities which have gross income or gross expenditure exceeding £100,000 in the current year or either of the preceding two years must have an audit. There is no exemption for very small charities, so all charities have to have some form of external scrutiny. An independent examiner should be "...an independent person who is reasonably believed by the trustees to have the requisite ability and practical experience to carry out a competent examination of the accounts." There are no further guidelines issued on the selection of independent examiners, so the guidance set out by the Charity Commissioners for charities in England and Wales may be useful in this respect. This is discussed more fully in Chapter 9.

The regulations applying to the appointment and removal of independent examiners are the same as those relating to auditors, as described above. Similarly, the smae provisions apply to resignations and the independent examiner has the same rights of access to information and explanations.

In his report the independent examiner has to state whether, to the best of his knowledge and belief and in accordance with the information and explanations given to him, the balance sheet and income and expenditure account and notes thereon, or the statement of balances and receipts and payments account and notes thereon, have been properly prepared from the records of the charity. In addition he has to state whether the accounts are in agreement with the records and comply with the regulations and the charity's founding deed.

The independent examiner shall also consider whether the trustees' report is consistent with the accounts and state in his report if there is any inconsistency.

The independent examiner shall also state if proper accounting records have not been kept or if he has not received all the information and explanations he considered necessary.

Example Independent Examiner's report to an unincorporated Scottish charity

REPORT OF THE INDEPENDENT EXAMINER
TO THE TRUSTEES OF
THE HIGHLANDS DEVELOPMENT TRUST

I have examined the [accounts] [account and statement] on pages ... to ... which have been prepared on the basis of the accounting policies set out on page...

Respective Responsibilities of Trustees and Examiner

The trustees of the charity are responsible for the preparation of accounts; they consider that the audit requirement under regulation 7 (1) of The Charities Accounts (Scotland) Regulations 1992 does not apply. I have been appointed under regulation 8 (1) of those Regulations and report in accordance with regulation 8. It is my responsibility to examine the accounts, without performing an audit, and to report to the trustees.

Basis of Examiner's Statement

This report is in respect of an examination carried out under regulation 8. An examination includes a review of the accounting records kept by the charity trustees and a comparison of the accounts presented with those records. It also includes a review of the accounts and making such enquiries as are necessary for the purposes of this report. The procedures undertaken do not constitute an audit.

Examiner's Statement

To the best of my knowledge and belief, the [balance sheet and income and expenditure account and notes thereon] [statement of balances and receipts and payments account and notes thereon] have been properly prepared from the records of the charity and are in agreement therewith. The accounts comply with The Charities Accounts (Scotland) Regulations 1992 and with the founding deed.

Whistleblowing

There are no whistleblowing obligations on auditors or independent examiners in the charity legislation. Auditors would need to consider whether the matter was in the public interest and would therefore report the matter to the Scottish Charities Office. Additional guidance on this area is contained in the Audit Practice Note for Charities being issued by the Auditing Practices Board. The Law Reform (Miscellaneous Provisions) (Scotland) Act 1990 gave the Lord Advocate significant additional powers in relation to the investigation of abuse in charities. The Scottish Charities Office handle enquiries in the first instance.

Glossary of Terms

Specific terminology and meanings are given in the Scottish legislation:

Body	Recognised body meaning a Scottish charity, i.e. a body which has gained recognition as charitable from the Inland Revenue.
Founding deed	The governing instrument being the constitution or rules of the organisation.
Gross income	Total of its income from all sources that is required in the terms of the regulations to be recorded in the income and expenditure account. This excludes income to permanent endowment funds, but includes gains on the disposal of fixed assets and investments.
Gross expenditure	Total of its expenditure on all purposes that is required in the terms of the regulations to be recorded in the income and expenditure account.
Gross receipts	Total of the sums received from all sources after deducting the proceeds, if any, of the sale of investments and the sale of assets and receipts in respect of a permanent endowment fund.
Permanent Endowment	This is a fund which must be held permanently although its constituent assets may change from time to time.
Designated Fund	This is a fund which has been allocated or designated for specific purposes by a charity.

NORTHERN IRELAND

Charities are not obliged to register with a regulatory body in Northern Ireland and there is no equivalent of the Charity Commission. Recognition of a charity by the Inland Revenue is generally accepted as evidence of charitable status. Charities are regulated in Northern Ireland by the Department of Health and Social Services through the Charities Branch of the Voluntary Activity Unit.

Charitable companies have to follow company legislation, which in Northern Ireland is the Companies (Northern Ireland) Acts and the Companies (Northern Ireland) Orders 1982 and 1986. This means in practice that companies in Northern Ireland follow the same regime as companies elsewhere in the UK. The audit and accounting requirements are the same.

The legislation under which unincorporated charities operate is the Charities Act (Northern Ireland) 1964 and the Charities (Northern Ireland) Order 1987. At present there is no audit requirement. Legislation is proposed to cover the audit and accounting aspects for unincorporated charities. This legislation proposes the following:

◆ audit required for all charities with gross income exceeding £250,000

◆ audit if required by the Department if gross income between £100,000 and £250,000

- ◆ independent examination by qualified accountant if not audited and gross income between £100,000 and £250,000
- ◆ independent examination by a suitable person if gross income less than £100,000
- ◆ no external review if gross income less than £10,000
- ◆ the form and content of accounts should follow best practice, e.g. SORP
- ◆ annual report will be required
- ◆ duty to establish and maintain an effective system of internal controls
- ◆ no obligation to submit accounts to a central file, but to submit accounts on request to the department and to any member of the public (with limited exceptions where security of staff or beneficiaries may be jeopardised)

It should be remembered that the SORP represents best practice for all charities unless thay are covered by another specialised SORP. Charities in Northern Ireland should therefore be following the SORP, whether incorporated or not. The SORP has immediate effect, so charities should follow this now.

APPENDIX I

Checklist for the Notes to the Accounts

This may be used as a checklist for the compilation of the notes to the accounts for most charities. Charities do need to also consider matters arising from company legislation and accounting standards where these apply. You should also consider whether there is anything that is unclear from the primary financial statements; give further explanation in the notes. You may also need to disclose additional matters to satisfy funding requirements.

Notes are only required where there is a material amount to disclose, either for the current or preceding year. The exception to this is the case of trustee remuneration and expenses, where a note stating that there was none should still be included.

The checklist is cross-referenced to the SORP, referring to the paragraph number in the SORP after the item.

		yes	n/a
1. Accounting Policies (para 35)			
1.1	follow accounting standards and SORP	☐	☐
1.2	basis for including voluntary income such as donations and legacies	☐	☐
1.3	basis for including grants receivable and treatment of grants for the purchase of fixed assets	☐	☐
1.4	basis of accounting for grants payable	☐	☐
1.5	the basis for the analysis of costs between direct charitable expenditure, support costs, fundraising and publicity costs and management and administration of the charity	☐	☐
1.6	income and expenditure on specialised activities, e.g. research	☐	☐
1.7	valuation of investment assets and how income therefrom is treated	☐	☐
1.8	treatment of realised and unrealised gains and losses	☐	☐
1.9	valuation, capitalisation and depreciation policies for fixed assets	☐	☐
1.10	netted off expenses and related income	☐	☐
1.11	subscriptions for life membership	☐	☐
1.12	stocks of goods or materials	☐	☐
1.13	commitments not yet met, and the need for designated funds	☐	☐
1.14	explanation of restricted and unrestricted funds, capital funds	☐	☐
2. Incoming Resources			
2.1	Additional analysis of the incoming resources (para 88)	☐	☐

		yes	n/a
2.2	Grant income – description of sources of material grants by category (para 120)	☐	☐
2.3	Incoming resources subject to pre-conditions which cannot be met should be explained (para 101)	☐	☐
2.4	Deferred income should be explained, with movements between accounting periods analysed (para 103)	☐	☐
2.5	Entitlement to legacies not included in the accounts with an estimate of the amount receivable (para 106)	☐	☐
2.6	Investment income – analysis of gross income by investment category (para 128)	☐	☐
2.7	Netted off incoming resources – reason for netting off, together with gross income and expenditure, if material (para 133)	☐	☐
2.8	Intangible income – details of intangible income included in SOFA (para 109)	☐	☐

3. Expenditure

		yes	n/a
3.1	"Natural" classification of expenditure may be shown to support the "functional" classification in the SOFA (para 136)	☐	☐
3.2	Grants payable – for grants to institutions disclose the recipient and total grants made to them in the financial year for the largest 50 grants where these are over £1,000. For grants to individuals, disclose the aggregate value and number of grants. (paras 137 to 139)	☐	☐
3.3	Analysis of all the major items included in support costs (para 152)	☐	☐
3.4	Analysis of all the major components of the total cost of managing and administering the charity (para 153)	☐	☐

4. Staff Emoluments

		yes	n/a
4.1	The total emoluments – remuneration and benefits in kind as defined for tax purposes – for all employees. Average number of employees in year. (para 160)	☐	☐
4.2	Employees receiving emoluments of £40,000 and more need to be disclosed in bands of £10,000 (para 161)	☐	☐

5. Auditors' Remuneration

		yes	n/a
5.1	Auditors' remuneration – separately showing amounts paid for audit and other services. Other services should be specified i.e accountancy, consultancy etc. (para 162)	☐	☐
	Same requirment if an independent examiner is reporting on the accounts. Disclose total for group if consolidated accounts prepared.	☐	☐

yes   _n/a_

6. Ex-gratia payments

6.1 Ex-gratia payments – total amount or value of any ex-
gratia payments, with details of any authority from
Charity Commissioners or court. (para 164)   ☐   ☐

7. Transfers

7.1 Transfers between funds should be explained (para 78)

7.2 Material transfers out of and allocations to designated
funds should be supported by a narrative explanation of
the nature of the transfer or alloxcation and the reason for it.   ☐   ☐

8. Fund Accounting

8.1 Endowment funds – analysis between permanent
endowment and expendable endowment; explanation of
initial gift and changes in funds (para 75)   ☐   ☐

8.2 Further explanation of the funds; for example, a more
detailed breakdown of the total restricted funds into
various specified funds; an analysis of unrestricted funds
into general funds and various designated funds (para 36
and para 43)   ☐   ☐

8.3 Analysis of assets and liabilities representing the various
funds, indicating whether the assets are sufficient for the
fulfilment of the purpose and that the assets are held in a
suitable form given the timescale of the activity (para 36 (a))   ☐   ☐

8.4 The purpose of designated funds (para 201)   ☐   ☐

9. Subsidiaries and Trading

9.1 The name of each subsidiary undertaking and particulars
of the charity's interest (para 58)   ☐   ☐

9.2 Additional information in notes as required to ensure that
the assets and liabilities and transactions of the charity can
be distinguished from those of the charity. Need to be able
to identify charity's direct charitable expenditure,
fundraising and pubicity costs and the costs of managing
and administering the charity. Minimum would be the
turnover and results of the subsidiary. (para 60)   ☐   ☐

9.3 Full trading results if the SOFA only showed net income
from trading (para 65 and para 123)   ☐   ☐

9.4 Funds retained by subsidiaries other than funds used in
carrying out the charity's main objects should be identified
in a note if not on the face of the balance sheet e.g. as
"non-charitable trading funds" (para 42)   ☐   ☐

	yes	*n/a*

9.5   Subsidiary not consolidated – reason and the amount of
investment, name of subsidiary, the charity's interest, how
activities relate to those of the charity, together with the
aggregate amount of capital and reserves if material and
summary of the profit and loss account, if material. Details
of any qualification in the audit report (para 59)   ☐ ☐

9.6   Charity's interests in associated undertakings, whether
consolidated or not, together with name of the undertaking.
(para 61 and 67)   ☐ ☐

9.7   Associated undertakings not consolidated – details of
name, charity's interest, aggregate capital and reserves,
if material, turnover and result for year, if material.   ☐ ☐

10. Fixed Assets

10.1   Where material, resources used for the purchase of tangible
fixed assets (or released from the disposal of fixed assets)
so as to increase/decrease the net movement in funds for
the year to show the net movement in funds available for
future activities. Note to be shown immediately after the
SOFA. (para 86)   ☐ ☐

10.2   Realised gains and losses arising on disposal of fixed
assets for charity use – explanation if material (para 130)   ☐ ☐

10.3   Tangible fixed assets – note setting out cost or valuation,
depreciation and net book value. Should distinguish between
assets for direct charitable use and other (para 183)   ☐ ☐

10.4   Revaluation of fixed assets – date and basis of valuation.
Name and qualification of person making the valuation,
where appropriate, e.g.property (para 175)   ☐ ☐

10.5   Details of any uncapitalised fixed assets, setting out age
and scale of the assets, insured value and what use is made
of them (para 187)   ☐ ☐

10.6   Tangible fixed assets for use by the charity to be divided
into categories: freehold land and buildings, leasehold
land and buildings, plant and machinery, including motor
vehicles, fixtures, fittings and equipment and payments on
account and assets in course of construction. Changes in
values, depreciation and reconciliation of opening and
closing net book values to be shown, (para 171)   ☐ ☐

11. Investments

11.1   Historical cost of investments should be disclosed (para 194)   ☐ ☐

		yes	*n/a*

11.2 Analysis of investment assets between investment properties, listed investments, subsidiaries, other unlisted securities, cash held as part of investment portfolio, other. Further analysis should show the UK and non-UK investments. Further information should be given on the structure of the portfolio. (paras 195 and 196) ☐ ☐

11.3 Investment funds – the fund to which the investment belongs should be clear (i.e. restricted, unrestricted, endowment). If the Trustee Investments Act applies, then the value of investments allotted to each range should be included (paras 197 and 198) ☐ ☐

12. Gifts in Kind

12.1 Undistributed assets held at year end (and not in the accounts) with a description of the items and an estimate of their value (para 107) ☐ ☐

12.2 Voluntary help (if not in trustees' report) (para 110) ☐ ☐

13. Debtors

13.1 Analysis into trade debtors, amounts owed by subsidiaries and associated undertakings, other debtors, prepayments and accrued income (para 171 b) ☐ ☐

13.2 Separate disclosure of loans made interest free or at a concessionary rate made in the furtherance of the charity's objects, showing the amounts involved and the rate of interest. (para 140) ☐ ☐

13.3 Debtors recoverable after more than one year should be disclosed in aggregate (para 141) ☐ ☐

14. Liabilities

14.1 Creditors – analysis into loans, bank overdrafts, trade creditors, amounts owed to subsidiary and associated undertakings, taxes, other creditors, accruals, deferred income (para 172) ☐ ☐

14.2 Secured loans – if the charity has taken out loans which are secured on charity assets, then the amount of the loan and the asset given as security must be disclosed (para 208) ☐ ☐

14.3 Guarantees – details of any guarantees given by the charity and conditions under which guarantee might be called upon (para 202) ☐ ☐

14.4 Contingent liabilities – nature of contingency, what might determine the outcome and an estimate of the financial effect (para 207) ☐ ☐

yes   *n/a*

15. Commitments

15.1   Particulars of all material commitments in respect of
specific charitable projects not provided for in the accounts
should be disclosed to show the amount involved, when
the commitments are likely to be met and the movements
on commitments previously reported (para 199)

☐   ☐

15.2   Particulars of all other material binding commitments
should also be disclosed e.g.operating leases (para 199)

☐   ☐

15.3   Particulars of all material charitable commitments
accrued as liabilities should be disclosed to include the
amount charged as expenditure for the year, when each
payment is likely to be made and the movement on any
previously accrued commitment (para 200)

☐   ☐

15.4   Charitable commitments only to be funded from future
income will not be accrued, but should be disclosed with
an explanation of the relationship between the income
and expenditure (para 145)

☐   ☐

15.5   Expenditure authorised but not contracted may be
recognised through a transfer of funds into designated
funds, with an explanatory note to describe the prupose
(para 146)

☐   ☐

16.   Connected Persons

16.1   Connected persons – details of any material transactions,
contracts or other arrangements with any connected
person (para 154)

☐   ☐

16.2   Trustees' remuneration – direct or indirect payment of
remuneration to trustees with source and amount. The f
act of no remuneration should be stated (para 157)

☐   ☐

16.3   Trustee expenses – the aggregate of expenses reimbursed
to all trustees, the type of expense (e.g. travel) and the
number of trustees receiving expenses. The fact that no
expenses paid to trustees should be stated (para 158)

☐   ☐

16.4   Indemnity insurance – the type and cost of any
indemnity insurance funded by the charity (para 159)

☐   ☐

REFERENCE MATERIALS

Legislation

Available from HMSO through their bookshops, certain other bookshops or by mail order from:

HMSO Publications Centre
P O Box 276
London SW8 5DT

Tel: 0171 873 9090
Fax: 0171 873 8200

The Charities Act 1993

The Charities (Accounts and Reports) Regulations 1995 (SI 1995 No. 2724)

Charity Accounts and Reports Core Guide - a combination of guidance from the Home Office, Part VI of the Charities Act 1993 (updated for the changed thresholds) and the accounting regulations.

Law Reform (Miscellaneous Provisions) (Scotland) Act 1990

The Charities Accounts (Scotland) Regulations 1992

Guidance

Available from the Charity Commission from any of their offices:

St Alban's House
57/60 Haymarket
London SW1Y 4QX
0171 210 4477

Woodfield House
Tangier
Taunton
Somerest TA1 4BL
01832 345000

2nd Floor
20 Kings Parade
Queen's Dock
Liverpool L3 4DQ
0151 703 1500

Accounting by Charities: Statement of Recommended Practice

Accounting for the Smaller Charity

Accruals Accounting for the Smaller Charity

Guidance on the Carrying Out of an Independent Examination

Charities Accounts Helpline at Charity Commission: 0151 703 1570

Available from the Institute of Chartered Accountants in England and Wales

Charities Audit Practice Note published by the Auditing Practices Board (APB)

INDEX

Accountant's report 11,21,22

Accounting policies 83,97,121,123,184

Accounting records 15-16

Accounting regulations . 11,15,23-24,39,172

Accruals basis of accounting 11,74-85

Analytical review 144,161,168-169

Annual accounts 16-17,172

Annual report 23-38,58-60,75-77,178

Annual review 36-37

Appropriations 172

Assets

   – analysis of 104,105,134

   – basis of valuation 11,116

   – revaluation 27,75,90,112,187

Audit Practice Note for Charities 138,181

   Audit requirement . 15,19,21,22,138,171

Auditor's

   – duties 139-140,179

   – report 146-148,149-150

   – resignation 153

Branches 51-52

Breach of trust 42,142,143

Capital 11,40-41

Cashflow statement 118

Charitable companies

   – form of accounts 18,21,139

   – audit requirements 15,18,21,22

Charity Commission – powers 15

Commitments 136,189

Compilation report 11,21,22

Contingent liabilities 174,188

Connected charities 54

Connected persons

   – definition 54-55

   – transactions with 54-55

Consolidated accounts 110-113,
   118-119,145

Creditors 84,102,116,132

Debtors 84,102,116,132,188

Deferred income 47-48

Depreciation 121

Designated funds ... 11,42,104,105,121,182

Direct charitable expenditure 11,44

Directors 34-36

Donated goods 87,88,122

Donated services 49

Endowments 11,40-41

Ex–gratia payment 186

Expendable endowment 11,42

Expenditure analysis 44-46,141,185

Financial Reporting Standard 3 (FRS 3) .. 11

Financial statements 12,121

Fixed assets

   – purchase 12,56,187

   – classification 55-56,84,116,187

   – revaluation 55-56,187

   – grant funded 187

Fund accounting 41,42,186

Fundraising and publicity costs 12,110

Funds – types 112

General funds 12,43

Gifts in kind 48-49,143-144,188

Going concern 144-145

Governing document 12

Grants payable 52

Grants received for the purchase
   of fixed assets 44,46-47

Gross income 12,20,182

Group accounts 50,120,134

Guarantees 27,64,174,188

Housing associations 17,139

Income and expenditure account 12

Incoming resources 12,43,110,126,140-
   141,184-185

Indemnity insurance 54,136,145

Independent examination

   – general directions 19-20,158-163

   – guidance 158

   – work programme 167-170

Independent examiner

   – duties 13,157-158

   – report 61,163-164,180,181

   – selection of 164-165

   – appointment 180

   – engagement letter 165-166

– liability of 166-167
Industrial and Provident Societies 139
Intangible income 49,143
Investments
– classification 102
– revaluation 102
– historical cost 102,187

Land transactions 154
Legacies 41,184,185
Life subscriptions 48

Management and administration costs ... 13,
110
Mortgages 154-155

Natural classification of costs 45,100,124
Netting off 41
Northern Irish Charities 182-183
Permanent endowment 13,42,182
Post balance sheet events 162,169
Professional indemnity 166-167

Realised gains and losses 184,187
Receipts and payments account 13,
57-73,148-149
Recognised body 178
Registered auditor 13
Remuneration
– staff 99
– auditors 136,185
– independent examiner 172
Restricted funds 13,42,84,104,
10,121,134,141
Revaluations 52-53,145

Scottish charities 13,171-182

Secured loans 188
SORP see Statement of
Recommended Practice
Special trusts 42,55
Staff costs 99,121,126
Staff emoluments 53-54,82,98,185
Statement of assets
and liabilities 13,64,68-73
Statement of Financial Activities(SOFA) .....
13,40,78-79,88-91
Statement of Recommended
Practice (SORP) 14,25-27
Stock 116,121,136
Subsidiary 49-51,110,186-187
Summarised accounts 37-38,155-156
Summary income and
expenditure account 56,92,93,114
Support costs 14,45

Tangible fixed assets 128
Tax recoverable 52
Total expenditure 14,20,100,110
Trading 110,186-187
Transfers 43-44,112,126,143,186
Trustee remuneration and expenses 53,
84,99,136,145
Trustee responsibilities 61,145-146

Unrealised gains or losses 53,56,92,
94,114,172
Unrestricted funds 14,42
Universities 18,139

Voluntary income 121
Volunteers 26,49

Whistleblowing........................150-153,181